THE

LAST NINETY DAYS OF THE WAR

IN

NORTH-CAROLINA.

BY

CORNELIA PHILLIPS SPENCER.

NEW-YORK:
WATCHMAN PUBLISHING COMPANY,
W. H. CHASE, PUBLISHING AGENT
1866.

BROADFOOT PUBLISHING COMPANY
WILMINGTON, NORTH CAROLINA
1993

"Fine Books Since 1970."

BROADFOOT PUBLISHING COMPANY
1907 Buena Vista Circle
Wilmington, North Carolina 28405

THIS BOOK IS PRINTED ON ACID-FREE PAPER

ISBN No. 1-56837-049-0

TO THE

Hon. D. L. Swain, LL.D.,

AT WHOSE SUGGESTION IT WAS UNDERTAKEN, AND BY WHOSE
INVALUABLE ADVICE, ENCOURAGEMENT, AND ASSIST-
ANCE IT HAS BEEN COMPLETED, THIS BOOK
IS MOST RESPECTFULLY
DEDICATED.

PREFACE.

THE papers on the LAST NINETY DAYS OF THE WAR IN NORTH-CAROLINA, which originally appeared in the New-York WATCHMAN, and are now presented in book form, were commenced with no plan or intention of continuing them beyond two or three numbers. The unexpected favor with which they were received led to their extension, and finally resulted in their republication.

To do justice to North-Carolina, and to place beyond cavil or reproach the attitude of her leaders at the close of the great Southern States Rights struggle—to present a faithful picture of the times, and a just judgment, whether writing of friend or foe, has been my sole object. Slight as these sketches are, they may claim at least the merit of truth, and this, I am persuaded, is no slight recommendation with the truth-loving people of North-Carolina.

CORNELIA PHILLIPS SPENCER
(1825-1908)

The Last Ninety Days of the War, Cornelia Phillips Spencer's first published book was written at the request of her dear friend David Lowry Swain. LLD, who served three terms as governor of North Carolina prior to accepting the presidency of the University of North Carolina at Chapel Hill. Governor Swain had known Cornelia since she was thirteen years old and, as her neighbor, mentor, and friend, was well aware of her inquisitive mind, keen perceptions, classical education, literary gifts, warmth, and common sense. Another North Carolina governor, Zebulon B. Vance also pegged Cornelia Spencer as something extra special and his quip has been repeated countless times. As the story goes—R.H. Battle remarked to Governor Vance that Cornelia was probably the smartest woman in North Carolina and the Governor replied: "She is the smartest woman in the State, yes, and the smartest man too."

This "smartest" North Carolina citizen merited honors in her own life-time, and after. At the University of North Carolina's Centennial in 1895, she was awarded an honorary doctor of laws, a first for a woman. In 1904, a dormitory was named for her at the North Carolina College for Women at Greensboro and the University of

North Carolina at Chapel Hill followed suit in 1924. In 1926, Mrs. Hope S. Chamberlain published a biography of her entitled *Old Days in Chapel Hill*. During World War II a Liberty ship built at Wilmington, North Carolina, was christened *Cornelia Phillips Spencer*. In 1949, the University of North Carolina Press published Phillips Russell's biography *The Woman Who Rang the Bell* and in 1953 *The Selected Papers of Cornelia Phillips Spencer*, which were introduced and edited by Louis R. Wilson.

Cornelia Phillips Spencer was born on 20 March 1825 in what was then the old Dutch section of Harlem in New York City. She was the only daughter of James and Judith (Julia) Vermeule Phillips. When Cornelia was still an infant her father accepted the chair of mathematics and natural philosophy at the University of North Carolina. Although Julia Phillips never fully felt at ease or at home in Chapel Hill, her daughter took to the sleepy little Southern town like the proverbial duck to water. She loved the intellectual stimulation that could be found in the groves of academe and she loved the groves and fields and flowers that were within an easy walk of the village.

Since both of Cornelia's parents were accomplished—her mother ran Mrs. Phillips School for Young Ladies—it is not surprising that their daughter displayed not only native ability but a genuine love of learning. Cornelia excelled at languages and without the least self consciousness could quote from memory Virgil and Horace and read French. She loved to read biography, history, essays, and poetry and felt it not the not the least bit unusual that she usually had several books "in progress" at once. Writing came naturally and although one of her poems, an ode, "Dear University," is still an official UNC song, its author modestly described herself as only a "versifier."

Although, Cornelia may sound like a 19th Century "Bluestocking," she was no stranger to the domestic arts. She took enormous pride in her ability to sew and manage a household on a limited budget. She was quite capable of staging memorable meals, such as the time she put on a community dinner for one hundred Black convicts who were building the railroad.

Cornelia also had a heart and hers was won by James Munroe Spencer, a graduate of the University. Magnus, as he was called, married Cornelia on 20 June 1855. The couple moved to Alabama where their daughter, Julia James Spencer, was born on 1 June 1859. Her proud father pronounced her a "June Bug" and the name stuck. June was destined to be Cornelia's only child and the joy of her life.

Shortly after June's first birthday, Magnus Spencer died of what was probably cancer of the spine. His widow and orphan returned to Chapel Hill and took up residence with the Phillipses.

Cornelia suffered deep depression during her early widowhood, a suffering that was compounded further by the realization that she was going deaf. A diary entry of June 1862 noted:

"My hearing is going, and with it my youth and hope and love....God in His Providence has brought me back here [Chapel Hill] to sit among the ruins of happiness, to sit here, and look on and remember."

Of course, being a mere "on-looker" was just not a part of Cornelia's makeup and she soon was emotionally involved with the progress of the war and the Southern States Rights Struggle. When Kilpatrick's cavalry, a 4,000 man vanguard of Sherman's Army arrived in Chapel Hill, Cornelia had an opportunity to be an eyewitness to the conduct of a conquering army and she also had a chance to demonstrate her loyalty to old friends. Brigadier General Smith D. Atkins was in charge of the forces and one of his first steps was to pay a call upon the University president, Governor Swain. Eleanor "Ellie" Swain happened to be present when the General and her father met and it literally was love at first sight. A very visible whirlwind three week courtship ensued that had all of Chapel Hill agog. The courting even included daily serenades from the regimental band. After General Atkins was ordered to another post, Ellie announced her intentions to marry the Yankee. Chapel Hill chose to boycott the wedding, but Cornelia made a point to be there. It was Swain, of course, who convinced Cornelia to write *The Last Ninety Days of the War* and her dedication was one more reminder that the author was not afraid to go public with her esteem for the former governor, who had become unpopular because of his family's connections with General Atkins.

After her father's death in 1867, Cornelia was forced to open a boarding house, a fate that was all too common for Southern women during the difficult times following the war. In 1868, it was announced that the University would be closed. This action, which incensed Cornelia to the nth degree, literally shut down the town of Chapel Hill and resulted in unemployed professors—including Cornelia's own brother—accepting positions at other institutions.

The Republican Reconstruction government then opened the school under the authority of Rev. Solomon Poole. Cornelia had no time for the "radical" politics of the new president and took real pleasure in his failure to attract students back to the campus. The University was closed again in 1870. Cornelia now became an activist with a mission and she was destined to become living proof of Bulwer-Lytton's famous line " the pen is mightier than the sword." Cornelia used her influence and ability as a word smith to conduct an effective campaign to convince those in power that the University of North Carolina must be opened. On Cornelia's 50th birthday—20 March 1875—she received a telegram from Kemp B. Battle informing her that the North Carolina Legislature had passed a bill permitting the reorganization of the University. There could not have been a better birthday gift. Cornelia marched to the South Building, which housed the bell that had been silent for five years. She climbed to the belfry, took the rope, and rang and rang and rang the bell.

The woman "who rang the bell" was not just content to rest on her laurels. She continued to write "The Young Ladies Column" for the *North Carolina Presbyterian* as well as other articles written under the by-line "From Our Chapel Hill Correspondent" for other newspapers and magazines. It was routine to maintain a daily journal, conduct a voluminous correspondence, keep abreast of current affairs, and read new authors as well as old favorites. In 1888, her second full-length book, *First Steps in North Carolina History*, was published. A genuine interest in young people was one of the hallmarks of Cornelia's life and she was delighted when the time came for her to be a doting grandmother. Although she could not hear the voices of her loved ones, she could hold them, read to them, pick flowers with them, make their clothes, and write notes and letters.

Among the many words of wisdom that Cornelia Phillips Spencer wrote was the advice: "always leave a wide margin for the unexpected."

It is unlikely that she would ever have expected her last years would be spent in Cambridge, Massachusetts. But age and circumstance made it necessary for her to make a home with her daughter and son-in-law, James Lee Love, a professor at Harvard. She adjusted to her new home, but her heart never forgot her beloved Chapel Hill and she wrote: "Yes, the time comes when, whatever the show may have been, one is glad to go home."

Cornelia Phillips Spencer went home in March 1908 to be buried beside her parents in the Chapel Hill Cemetery. She had hoped that "when dead" to be remembered by two or three "in faithful remembrance." Generations of North Carolinians have admired her countless contributions to the State's history and education and have remembered her with pride.

Diane Cobb Cashman
October 1992
Wilmington, North Carolina

CONTENTS.

———◆———

CHAPTER XIII.

CHAPTER XIV.

CHAPTER XV.

CHAPTER XVI.

CHAPTER XVII.

CHAPTER XVIII.

APPENDIX.

THE LAST NINETY DAYS OF THE WAR

IN

NORTH-CAROLINA.

----•••----

CHAPTER I.

It will be long before the history of the late war can be soberly and impartially written. The passions that have been evoked by it will not soon slumber, and it is perhaps expecting too much of human nature, to believe that a fair and candid statement of facts on either side will soon be made. There is as yet too much to be forgotten—too much to be forgiven.

The future historian of the great struggle will doubtless have ample material at his disposal; but from a vast mass of conflicting evidence he will have to sift, combine, and arrange the grains of truth—a work to which few men of this generation are competent. But meanwhile there is much to be done in collecting evidence, especially by those who desire that justice shall be done to the South : and this evidence, it is to be hoped, will be largely drawn from *private* sources. History has in general no more invaluable and irrefragable witnesses for the truth than are to be found in the journals, memoranda, and private correspondence of the prominent and influential men who either acted in, or were compelled to remain quiet observers of the events of their day. Especially will this be found to be the case when posterity shall sit in judgment on the past four years in the South. From no other sources can so fair a representation be made of the conflicts of opinion, or of the motives of action in the time when madness seemed to rule the hour, when all individual and all State efforts for peace were powerless, when sober men were silenced, and when even the public press could hardly be considered free.

If it be true of the South in general, that even in the most excited localities warning voices were raised in vain, and that a strong undercurrent of good sense and calm reflection undoubtedly existed—overborne for a time by the elements of strife and revolution— more especially and with tenfold emphasis is it true of the State of North-Carolina.

> " Where we lay,
> Our chimneys were blown down : and, as they say,
> Lamentings heard i' the air ; strange screams of death ;
> And prophesying, with accents terrible,
> Of dire combustion, and confused events,
> New-hatched to the woful time."

That North-Carolina accepted a destiny which she

was unable to control, when she ranged herself in the war for Southern independence, is a fact which can not be disputed. And though none the less ardently did her sons spring to arms, and none the less generously and splendidly did her people sustain the great army that poured forth from her borders; though none the less patient endurance and obedience to the general government was theirs; yet it is also a fact, indisputable and on record, that North-Carolina was never allowed her just weight of influence in the councils of the Southern Confederacy, nor were the opinions or advice of her leading men either solicited or regarded. And therefore, nowhere as in the private, unreserved correspondence of her leading men, can her attitude at the beginning, her temper and her course all through, and her action at the close of the war, be so clearly and so fairly defined and illustrated, and shown to be eminently consistent and characteristic throughout.

The efforts made by North-Carolina, during the winter and spring of 1861, to maintain peace and to preserve the Union, were unappreciated, unsuccessful, and perhaps were not even generally known. In February of that year, two separate delegations left the State, appointed by her Legislature, each consisting of selections from her best citizens—one for Washington City and the other for Montgomery, Alabama. Judge Ruffin, Governor Morehead, Governor Reid, D. M. Barringer, and George Davis were accredited to the Peace Convention at Washington; Governor Swain and Messrs. Bridgers and Ransom to the Convention at Montgomery, to meet the delegations expected to convene there from the other Southern States.

Neither of these delegations, however, were able to effect any thing. They were received with courtesy, respect, and attention on each side, but nothing was done. The Peace Convention at Washington was a failure—why or how, has never been clearly shown. If one or other of the distinguished gentlemen who formed the North-Carolina delegation would commit an account of the mission to writing, he would be doing the State good service. I would venture to suggest it to Judge Ruffin, whose appearance there was said to have been in the highest degree venerable and impressive, and his speech *for the Union* and for the Old Flag most eloquent and affecting.

The expected delegations from the other Southern States to Montgomery failed to arrive, and North-Carolina was there alone, and could only look on. The provisional government for such of the States as had already seceded was then acting, and the general Confederate government was in process of organization. Our delegates were treated with marked courtesy, and were invited to attend the secret sessions of the Congress, which, however, they declined. North-Carolina stood there alone ; and as she maintained an attitude of calm and sad deprecation, she was viewed with distrust and suspicion by all extremists, and was taunted with her constitutional slowness and lack of chivalric fire. The moderation and prudence of her counsels were indeed but little suited to the fiery temper of that latitude. Too clearly, even then, she saw the end from the beginning; but what was left for her, when the clouds lowered and the storm at last broke, but to stand where the God of nature had placed her, and where affection and interest both inclined her—*in* the South and *with* the South? To that standard, then, her brave sons flocked, in obedience to her summons; for them and for their safety and success were her prayers and tears given; for their comfort and subsistence every nerve was strained in the mortal struggle that followed; and their graves will be forever hallowed—none the less, I repeat, that from the first the great body of her people and the best and most clearsighted of her public men deprecated the whole business of secession, and with sad prevision foretold the result.

If history shall do her justice, the part played by North-Carolina all through this mournful and bloody drama will be found well worthy of careful study.

The quiet and self-reliant way in which, when she found remonstrance to be in vain, she went to her inevitable work; the foresight of her preparations; the thoroughness of her equipments; the splendor of her achievements on the battle-field; her cheerful and patient yielding to all lawful demands of the general government; her watchful guard against unlawful encroachments, as the times grew more and more lawless; her silence, her modesty, and her efficiency—were all strikingly *North-Carolinian*. Not one laurel would she appropriate from the brow of a sister State—nay, the blood shed and the sufferings endured in the common cause but cement the Southern States together in dear-er bonds of affection. No word uttered by a North-Carolinian in defense or praise of his own mother, can be construed as an attempt to exalt her at the expense of others. But I am speaking now of North-Carolina alone, and my principal object will be to present the closing scenes of the war, as they appeared within some part of her borders, and to make a plain record of her action therein—a sketch which may afford valu_able memoranda to the future historian.

Much of the energy and the efficiency displayed by the State in providing for the exigencies of war, were due to the young man whom she chose for her Governor, in August, 1862. Governor Vance was one of the people—one of the soldiers—and came from the camp to the palace undoubtedly the most popular man in the State. A native of Buncombe county, he had been in a great measure the architect of his own fortunes. Possessing unrivaled abilities as a popular speaker, he had made his way rapidly in the confidence of the brave and free mountaineers of Western Carolina, and was a member of the United States House of Represent_atives for the term ending at the inauguration of President Lincoln. He used all his influence most ardently to avert the disruption of the Union, down to the time when the Convention of May, 1861, passed the ordinance of secession. Then, following the fortunes of his own State, he threw himself with equal ardor into the ranks of her army. Volunteering as private in one of the first companies raised in Buncombe, he was soon elected captain, and thence rose rapidly to be Colonel of the Twenty-sixth regiment. His further military career was closed by his being elected Governor in 1862, by an overwhelming vote, over the gentleman who was generally considered as the candidate of the secession party. We were, indeed, all secessionists then; but those who were defined as " *original seces-sionists* "—men who invoked and cheered on the movement and the war—were ever in a small minority in this State, both as to numbers and to influence. Governor Vance was elected because he *had been* a strong Union man, and *was* a gallant soldier—two qualifications which some of our Northern brethren can not admit as consistent or admirable in one and the same true character, but which together constituted the strongest claim upon the confidence and affection of North-Carolina.

Governor Vance's career from the first was marked by devotion to the people who had distinguished him, and by a determination to do his duty to *them* at all hazards. This is not the place, nor have I the material for such a display of Governor Vance's course of action as would do him deserved justice; but this I may say, that his private correspondence, if ever it shall be published, will endear him still more to the State which he loved, and to the best of his ability served.

His employment of a blockade-runner to bring in clothing for the North-Carolina troops was a noble idea, and proved a brilliant success.* If he had done

* Since the publication of the above, I have been informed by Governor Vance that the first suggestion of this plan was due to Gen. J. G. Martin alone. He was at that time Adjutant-General of the State, and at a consultation held by Governor Vance soon after his entrance upon office, to devise ways and means for providing

nothing else in his official career to prove himself worthy to be our Governor, this alone would be sufficient. It matters but little as to the amount, great or small, of Confederate money spent in this service. It is all gone now ; but the substantial and incalculable good that resulted at the time from this expenditure, can neither be disputed nor forgotten. For two years his swift-sailing vessels, especially the A. D. Vance, escaped the blockaders, and steamed regularly in and out of the port of Wilmington, followed by the prayers and anxieties of our whole people. "The Advance is in!" was a signal for congratulations in every town in the State; for we knew that another precious cargo was safe, of shoes, and blankets, and cloth, and medicines, and cards. And so it was that when other brave men went barefoot and ill-clad through the winter storms of Virginia, our own North Carolina boys were well supplied, and their wives and little ones at home were clothed, thanks to our Governor and to our God.

I have seen tears of thankfulness running down the cheeks of our soldiers' wives on receiving a pair of these cards, by which alone they were to clothe and procure bread for themselves and their children. And they never failed to express their sense of what they owed to their Governor. "God bless him!" they would cry, "for thinking of it. And God *will* bless him."

One striking evidence of the fullness and efficiency

---

for our soldiers, Gen. Martin suggested and advocated the employment of a blockade-runner. It was a bold and happy thought, and as boldly and happily carried out by Governor Vance.

of these supplies I can not refrain from giving, as it occurred at the close of the war, when our resources, it might be supposed, were utterly exhausted. It will also serve to show what manner of man Governor Vance was, in more ways than one.

In February, 1865, the attention of óur people was called to the condition of the Federal prisoners at Salisbury. The officer in charge of them may or may not have been as he is represented. Time will bring the truth to light. But it was alleged against him, that he would not only do nothing himself for the unhappy prisoners under his care, but would allow no private interference for their comfort. The usual answer of all such men, when appealed to on the score of common humanity, was, " What business have these Yankees here ?" This was deemed triumphant and unanswerable. That their food should be scanty and of poor quality was unavoidable when our own citizens were in want and our soldiers were on half-rations ; but sufficient clothing, kind attendance, and common decencies and comforts were, or might have been, extended to all within the bounds of our State. How far the Federal Government was itself responsible and criminal in this matter, by its refusal to exchange prisoners, future investigations will decide. The following extract of a letter from a prominent member of our last Legislature to a distinguished citizen, shows what the State of North-Carolina could and would have done for their relief :

"I called at Governor Vance's office, in the capitol, and found him sitting alone ; and though his desk was covered with papers and documents, these did not seem to engage his attention. He rather seemed to be in profound thought. He expressed himself pleased to see me, and proceeded to say that he had just seen a Confederate surgeon from Salisbury—mentioning his name—and was shocked at what he had heard of the condition of the Federal prisoners there. He went on to detail what he had heard, and testified deep feeling during the recital. He concluded by saying that he wished to see the State take some action on the subject. I assured him immediately how entirely I sympathized with him, and asked what relief it was in our power to bestow. He replied that the State had a full supply of clothing, made of English cloth, for our own troops, and that she had also a considerable quantity made of our own factory cloth. And further, that the State had also a very large supply of under-clothing, blankets, etc.; a supply of all which things might be dispensed to the prisoners, without trenching upon the comfort of our own troops. I told him that a resolution, vesting him with proper authority to act in the matter, could, I thought, be passed through the Legislature. That I thought it very desirable that such a resolution should be passed unanimously; and with a view to obviate objections from extreme men, it was better so to shape the resolution as to make it the means of obtaining reciprocal relief for our own prisoners at the North. This was done. The resolution requesting Governor Vance to effect an arrangement by which, in consideration of blankets, clothing, etc., to be distributed by the Federal Government to prisonners of war from North-Carolina, blankets, clothing, etc., in like quantity, should be distributed by the State of North-Carolina to the Federal prisoners at Salisbury, passed both houses, I think, without one dissentient voice, within the next day."

The letter-books of Governor Vance, it will be remembered, passed into the hands of the military authorities in May, 1865; and, under the order of General Schofield, were transmitted to the State Department at Washington. Whether they have been or are to be returned to the Executive Department of this State, to whom they properly belong, remains to be seen. A correspondent of the New-York press, who was allowed to examine them, remarks that " among much evil they exhibited *redeeming traits of character!*" that "the letters of Governor Vance to Mr. Secretary Seddon, of the War Department of Richmond, and to General Bradley Johnson, who had control of the prisoners at Salisbury, *urged* upon both these functionaries the immediate relief of the suffering prisoners, as alike dictated by humanity and policy." This correspondence, when it shall come to light, will show that the action of the executive was as prompt and decided as that of the legislative department of the State. Whatever may be said of the treatment of prisoners at Andersonville and elsewhere, it is certain that no efforts were spared on the part of the public authorities of North-Carolina, nor, we may add, of the community around Salisbury, to mitigate, as far as was possible, the inevitable horrors of war; and that our Governor, especially, exerted all the power and influence at his command to render immediate and effectual relief.

Governor Vance received no reply to his application to the Federal authorities. From General Bradley Johnson, at Salisbury, he received in reply a list of clothing and provisions then being received from the North for the prisoners; and a statement that they needed nothing but some tents, which Governor Vance was unable to send them.

The investigations of the Gee trial, held at Raleigh since the above was written, have served to substantiate all that I have said. What we could do, we were willing to do for our unhappy prisoners. But our own people, our own soldiers, were on the verge of starvation. Every effort was made by our authorities to induce the Northern Government to exchange, without effect. Their men died by thousands in our semitropical climate, because we were powerless to relieve them with either food or medicine. No one can read the testimony given at the Gee trial without a deep impression of the awful state of destitution among us. The country around Salisbury was stripped bare of provisions, and the railroads were utterly unfit for service. One of the witnesses stated that they had to take up the turn-outs to mend the road with. Writing now, at a distance of nearly two years, I can not recall the dark and hopeless days of that winter without a shudder. We knew the condition of those prisoners while we were mourning over the destitution of our own army. The coarse bread served at our own meagre repasts was made bitter by our reflections. A lady, writing from Salisbury, said : " I am much more concerned at the condition of these prisoners than at the advance of Sherman's army."

That North-Carolina had at least clothing to offer them was more than could be said for any other Southern State in that respect. She was probably worse off for provision than those south of her. She gave what she had. She did what she could.

CHAPTER II.

THE fall and winter of 1864–'5 were especially gloomy to our people. The hopes that had so long delusively buoyed up the Southern States in their desperate struggle against overwhelming odds were beginning to flag very perceptibly in every part of the Confederacy where people were capable of appreciating the facts of the situation. More especially, then, in North-Carolina, situated so near to the seat of war that false rumors, telegrams, and "reliable gentlemen" from the front had never had more than a very limited circulation here, and whose sober people never had been blinded or dazzled by the glare of false lights ; more especially here were there only gloomy outlooks for the year 1865, as it dawned.

In September, 1864, our representative Governor had written thus confidentially to his oldest and most warmly attached personal friend, a gentleman of the highest consideration in the State—a letter that needs neither introduction nor comment to secure it atten- tion:

"RALEIGH, September 22, 1864.

"I would be glad if I could have a long talk with you. I never before have been so gloomy about the condition of affairs. Early's defeat in the valley I consider as the turning-point in this campaign; and, confidentially, I fear it seals the fate of Richmond, though not immediately. It will require our utmost exertions to retain our footing in Virginia till '65 comes in. McClellan's defeat is placed among the facts, and abolitionism is rampant for four years more. The army in Georgia is utterly demoralized; and by the time President Davis, who has gone there, dis- plays again his obstinacy in defying public sentiment, and his ignorance of men in the change of command- ers, its ruin will be complete. They are now desert- ing by hundreds. In short, if the enemy pushes his luck till the close of the year, we shall not be offered any terms at all.

"The signs which discourage me more than aught else are the utter demoralization of the people. With a base of communication five hundred miles in Sher- man's rear, through our own country, not a bridge has been burned, not a car thrown from its track, nor a man shot by the people whose country he has deso- lated. They seem everywhere to submit when our armies are withdrawn. What does this show, my dear sir? It shows what I have always believed, that *the great popular heart* is not now, and never has been in this war. It was a revolution of the *Politicians*, not the *People ;* and was fought at first by the natural enthusiasm of our young men, and has been kept going by State and sectional pride, assisted by that bitterness of feeling produced by the cruelties and brutalities of the enemy.

"Still, I am not out of heart, for, as you know, I am of a buoyant and hopeful temperament. Things may come round yet. General Lee is *a great man*, and has the remnant of the best army on earth, bleeding, torn, and overpowered though it be. Saturday night may yet come to all of our troubles, and be followed by the blessed hours of rest. God grant it! 'Lord, I believe, help Thou mine unbelief' in final liberty and independence. I would fain be doing. How can I help to win the victory? What can I do? How shall I guide this suffering and much-oppressed Israel that looks to me through the tangled and bloody pathway wherein our lines have fallen? Duty called me to resist to the utmost the disruption of the Union. Duty calls me now to stand by the new union, 'to the last gasp with truth and loyalty.' This is my consolation. The beginning was bad: I had no hand in it. Should the end be bad, I shall, with God's help, be equally blameless.

"I hope when you come down, you will give yourself time to be with me a great deal.

"I am, dear sir, very truly yours,

"Z. B. VANCE."

The saddest forebodings of this letter, which would

have been echoed by many a failing heart in the State, were soon to be realized. By January, 1865, there was very little room left for "belief" of any sort in the ultimate success of the Confederacy. All the necessaries of life were scarce, and were held at fabulous and still increasing prices. The great freshet of January 10th, which washed low grounds, carried off fences, bridges, mills, and tore up railroads all through the central part of the State, at once doubled the price of corn and flour. Two destructive fires in the same month, which consumed great quantities of government stores at Charlotte and at Salisbury, added materially to the general gloom and depression. The very elements seemed to have enlisted against us. And soon, with no great surplus of food from the wants of her home population, North-Carolina found herself called upon to furnish supplies for two armies.

Early in January, an urgent and most pressing appeal was made for Lee's army; and the people, most of whom knew not where they would get bread for their children in three months' time, responded nobly, as they had always done to any call for "the soldiers." Few were the hearts in any part of the land that did not thrill at the thought that those who were fighting for us were in want of food. From the humble cabin on the hill-side, where the old brown spinning-wheel and the rude loom were the only breastworks against starvation, up through all grades of life, there were none who did not feel a deep and tender, almost heart-breaking solicitude for our noble soldiers. For them the last barrel of flour was divided, the last luxury in

homes that had once abounded was cheerfully surrendered.   Every available resource was taxed, every expedient of domestic economy was put in practice—as
indeed had been done all along ; but our people went
to work even yet with fresh zeal. I speak now of Central North-Carolina, where many families of the highest respectability and refinement lived for months on
corn-bread, sorghum, and peas ; where meat was seldom on the table, tea and coffee never ; where dried
apples and peaches were a luxury; where children
went barefoot through the winter, and ladies made
their own shoes, and wove their own homespuns ;
where the carpets were cut up into blankets, and win-
dow-curtains and sheets were torn up for hospital uses ;
where soldiers' socks were knit day and night, while
for home service clothes were twice turned, and
patches were patched again; and all this continually,
and with an energy and a cheerfulness that may well
be called *heroic*.

There were localities in the State where a few rich
planters boasted of having "never felt the war;"
there were ladies whose wardrobes encouraged the
blockade-runners, and whose tables were still heaped
with all the luxuries they had ever known. There
were such doubtless in every State in the Confederacy.
I speak not now of these, but of the great body of
our citizens—the *middle* class as to fortune, generally
the *highest* as to cultivation and intelligence—*these*
were the people who denied themselves and their little
ones, that they might be able to send relief to the gallant men who lay in the trenches before Petersburgh,

and were even then living on crackers and parched corn.

The fall of Fort Fisher and the occupation of Wilmington, the failure of the peace commission, and the unchecked advance of Sherman's army northward from Savannah, were the all-absorbing topics of discussion with our people during the first months of the year 1865. The tide of war was rolling in upon us. Hitherto our privations, heavily as they had borne upon domestic comfort, had been light in comparison with those of the people in the States actually invaded by the Federal armies ; but now we were to be qualified to judge, by our own experience, how far their trials and losses had exceeded ours. What the fate of our pleasant towns and villages and of our isolated farmhouses would be, we could easily read by the light of the blazing roof-trees that lit up the path of the advancing army. General Sherman's principles were well known, for they had been carefully laid down by him in his letter to the Mayor of Atlanta, September, 1864, and had been thoroughly put in practice by him in his further progress since. To shorten the war by increasing its severity : this was his plan—simple, and no doubt to a certain extent effective. But it is surely well worth serious inquiry and investigation on the part of those who decide these questions, and settle the laws of nations, how far the laws and usages of war demand and justify the entire ruin of a country and its unresisting inhabitants by the invading army ; or if those laws, as they are interpreted by the common-sense of civilized humanity, do indeed justify such a course, how far they are susceptible of change and improvement.

That the regulations which usually obtain in armies invading an enemy's country do at least permit every species of annoyance and oppression, tending to assist the successful prosecution of the war, to be exercised toward non-combatants, is unhappily testified by the annals of even modern and so-called Christian warfare. Especially are the evil passions of a brutal soldiery excited and inflamed where the inhabitants betake themselves to guerrilla or partisan warfare; and more especially and fatally in the case of long-protracted sieges, or the taking of a town by storm. The excesses committed by both the English and the French armies in the war of the Peninsula are recorded (and execrated) by their own generals, and are characterized by the historian as "all crimes which man in his worst excesses can commit—horrors so atrocious that their very atrocity preserves them from our full execration because it makes it impossible to describe them." Havoc and ruin have always accompanied invading armies to a greater or less degree, modified by the causes of the war, the character of the commanding officers, and the amount of discipline maintained.

A little more historical and political knowledge diffused among her people might have saved the South the unnecessarily bitter lesson she has received on this matter. Very, very few of the unthinking young men and women who clamored so madly for war four years ago, knew what fiend they were invoking. Few, very few of their leaders knew. Could the curtain that vailed the future have been lifted but for a moment before them, how would they have recoiled horror-stricken! But while admitting that in cases of very bitter national hatreds, ill-disciplined soldiery, and raw generals, excesses are allowed and defended, it is also the province of history to point with pride to those instances where veteran commanders, knowing well the horrors of war, seek to alleviate its miseries, and "seize the opportunities of nobleness," and, believing with Napier, that "discipline has its root in patriotism," do effectually control the armies they lead. Of such as these there are happily not a few great names whose humanity and generosity exhibited to the unfortunate inhabitants of the country they were traversing lend additional lustre to their fame as consummate soldiers. I shall, however, recall but one example to confirm this position—an example likely to be particularly interesting to Southerners as a parallel, and most striking as a contrast, to General Sherman's course in the South.

In the month of January, 1781, exactly eighty-four years before General Sherman's artillery trains woke the echoes through the heart of the Carolinas, it pleased God to direct the course of another invading army along much the same track; an army that had come three thousand miles to put down what was in truth "a rebellion;" an army stanch in enthusiastic loyalty to the government for whose rights it was contending; an army also in pursuit of retreating "rebels," and panting to put the finishing blow to a hateful secession, and whose commander endeavored to arrive at his ends by strategical operations very much resembling those which in this later day were crowned with success. Here the parallel ends. The country traversed then and now by invading armies was, eighty-four years ago, poor and wild and thinly settled. Instead of a single grand, deliberate, and triumphant march through a highly cultivated and un-defended country, there had been many of the undu-lations of war in the fortunes of that army—now pur-suing, now retreating—and finally, in the last hot chase of the flying (and yet triumphant) rebels from the southern to the northern border of North-Carolina, that invading army, to add celerity to its movements, voluntarily and deliberately destroyed all its baggage and stores, the noble and accomplished Commander-in-Chief himself setting the example. The inhabit-ants of the country, thinly scattered and unincum-bered with wealth, exhibited the most determined hostility to the invaders, so that if ever an invading army had good reason and excuse for ravaging and pillaging as it passed along, that army may surely be allowed it.

What was the policy of its commander under such circumstances toward the people of Carolina ?

I have before me now Lord Cornwallis's own order-book — truly venerable and interesting — bound in leather, with a brass clasp, the paper coarse and the ink faded, but the handwriting uncommonly good, and the whole in excellent preservation. A valuable relic in these days, when it is well to know what are the traits which go to make a true soldier, and how he may at least endeavor to divest war of its brutality. A few extracts will show what Cornwallis's principles were.

"Camp near Beattie's Ford,
January 28, 1781.

"Lord Cornwallis has so often experienced the zeal and good-will of the army, that he has not the smallest doubt that the officers and soldiers will most cheerfully submit to the ill conveniences that must naturally attend war so remote from water carriage and the magazines of the army. The supply of rum for a time will be absolutely impossible, and that of meal very uncertain. It is needless to point out to the officers the necessity of preserving the strictest discipline, and of preventing the oppressed people from suffering violence by the hands from whom they are taught to look for protection.

"To prevent the total destruction of the country and the ruin of his Majesty's service, it is necessary that the regulation in regard to the number of horses taken should be strictly observed. Major-General Leslie will be pleased to require the most exact obedience to this order from the officers commanding brigades and corps. The supernumerary horses that may from time to time be discovered will be sent to head quarters."

"Headquarters, Cansler's Plantation,
February 2, 1781.

"Lord Cornwallis is highly displeased that several houses have been set on fire to-day during the march— a disgrace to the army—and he will punish with the utmost severity any person or persons who shall be found guilty of committing so disgraceful an outrage. His Lordship requests the commanding officers of the corps will endeavor to find the persons who set fire to the houses this day."

"HEADQUARTERS, DOBBIN'S HOUSE,
February 17, 1781.

"Lord Cornwallis is very sorry to be obliged to call the attention of the officers of the army to the repeated orders against plundering, and he assures the officers that if their duty to their king and country, and their feeling for humanity, are not sufficient to enforce their obedience to them, he must, however reluctantly, make use of such power as the military laws have placed in his hands.

"Great complaints having been made of negroes straggling from the line of march, plundering and using violence to the inhabitants, it is Lord Cornwallis's positive orders that no negro shall be suffered to carry arms on any pretense, and all officers and other persons who employ negroes are desired to acquaint them that the provost-marshal has received orders to seize and shoot on the spot any negro following the army who may offend against these regulations.

"It is expected that captains will exert themselves to keep good order and prevent plundering. Should any complaint be made of the wagoners or followers of the army, it will be necessarily imputed to neglect on the part of the captains. Any officer who looks on with indifference, and does not do his utmost to prevent shameful marauding, will be considered in a more criminal light than the persons who commit these scandalous crimes, which must bring disgrace and ruin on his Majesty's service.

" All foraging parties will give receipts for the supplies taken by them."

> " HEADQUARTERS, FREELANDS, }
> February 28, 1781. }

MEMORANDUM.

" A watch found by the regiment of Bose. The owner may have it from the adjutant of that regiment on proving his property."

> " CAMP SMITH'S PLANTATION, }
> March 1, 1781. }

" BRIGADE ORDERS.

" It is Brigadier-General O'Hara's orders that the officers commanding companies cause an immediate inspection of the articles of clothing, etc., in the possession of the women in their companies, and an exact account taken thereof by the pay-sergeants; after which, their necessaries are to be regularly examined at proper intervals, and every article found in addition thereto burnt at the head of the company—except such as have been fairly purchased on application to the commanding officers and added to their former list by the sergeants as above. The officers are likewise ordered to make these examinations at such times, and in such manner as to prevent the women (supposed to be the source of infamous plundering*) from evading the purport of this order.

* 'Tis a thousand pities that a certain gallant major-general, late of the cav-

" A woman having been robbed of a watch, a black silk handkerchief, a gallon of peach brandy, and a shirt, and, as by the description, by a soldier of the Guards, the camp and every man's kit is to be immediately searched for the same by the officers of the brigade.

" Notwithstanding every order, every entreaty that Lord Cornwallis has given to the army, to prevent the shameful practice of plundering and distressing the country, and these orders backed by every effort that can have been made by Brigadier-General O'Hara, he is shocked to find that this evil still prevails, and ashamed to observe that the frequent complaints he receives from headquarters of the irregularity of the Guards particularly affect the credit of that corps. He therefore calls upon the officers, non-commissioned officers, and those men who are yet possessed of the feelings of humanity, and actuated by the principles of true soldiers, *the love of their country, the good of the service, and the honor of their own corps*, to assist with the same indefatigable diligence the General himself is determined to persevere in, in order to detect and punish all men and women so offending with the utmost severity of example."

Such was Lord Cornwallis's policy. What was the disposition toward him of the country through which he was passing? " So inveterate was the rancor of the inhabitants, that the expresses for the Commander-in-Chief were frequently murdered ; and the people,

alry service in General S.'s army, (now Minister to Chili,) could not have his attention drawn to this.

instead of remaining quietly at home to receive pay for the produce of their plantations, made it a practice to waylay the British foraging parties, fire their rifles from concealed places, and then fly to the woods." (Stedman's History.)

In all cases where the country people practice such warfare, retaliation by the army so annoyed is justified.   But even in Colonel Tarleton's (" bloody Tarleton's") command, Lord Cornwallis took care that justice should be done.   In Tarleton's own narrative we read :

" On the arrival of some country people, Lord Cornwallis directed Lieutenant-Colonel Tarleton to dismount his dragoons and mounted infantry, and to form them into a rank entire, for the convenient inspection of the inhabitants, and to facilitate the discovery of the villains who had committed atrocious outrages the preceding evening.   A sergeant and one private were pointed out, and accused of rape and robbery.   They were condemned to death by martial law.   The immediate infliction of this sentence exhibited to the army and manifested to the country the discipline and justice of the British General."

In Lee's Memoirs, we learn that on one occasion he captured on the banks of the Haw, in Alamance, two of Tarleton's staff, " who had been detained in *settling for the subsistence of the detachment.*"   What was the course of General Sherman's officers, eighty four years afterward, in the very same neighborhood, on the very same ground, let us now see.   " Look on this picture, then on that."

CHAPTER III.

In the first week of May, 1865, *after* the final surrender of General Johnston's army, and *after* General
Grant's proclamation of protection to private property,
Major-General Couch, with a detachment of some
twelve or fourteen thousand infantry, passing up the
main road from Raleigh to Greensboro, encamped on
a noble plantation, beautifully situated on both sides
of the Haw river, in Alamance county. Of the venerable owner of this plantation I might be pardoned if I
were to give more than a cursory notice; for, as a representative North-Carolinian, and identified for nearly
fifty years with all that is best in her annals and
brightest in her reputation at home and abroad, no
citizen in the State is regarded with more pride and
veneration than Judge RUFFIN. His claims to such
distinction, however, are not to be fairly exhibited

within the limits of such a sketch as this, though a
reference to his public services will have a significant
value in my present connection.

Judge Ruffin was born in 1786, graduated at Prince-
ton in 1806, was admitted to the bar in 1808, and
from the year 1813, when he first represented Hillsboro in the House of Commons, to the present time,
he has been prominently before the people of our
State, holding the highest offices within her gift with
a reputation for learning, ability, and integrity unsurpassed in our judicial annals.   In the year 1852, after
forty-five years of brilliant professional life, he resigned
the Chief-Justiceship, and, amid the applause and regret of all classes of his fellow-citizens, retired to the
quiet enjoyment of an ample estate acquired by his
own eminent labors, and to the society of a numerous
and interesting family.

The judicial ermine which Judge Ruffin had worn
for so many years not only shielded him from, but
absolutely forbade, all active participation in party
politics. He was, however, no uninterested observer
of the current of events. He had been warmly opposed to nullification in 1832, and was no believer in
the rights of peaceable secession in 1860.   In private
circles, he combated both heresies with all that " in-
exorable logic " which the London *Times* declared to
be characteristic of his judicial opinions on the law of
master and slave. He regarded the " sacred right of
revolution " as the remedy for the redress of insup-
portable grievances only. His opinions on these subjects were well known, when, in 1861, he was unex-

pectedly summoned by the Legislature to the head of
the able delegation sent by the State to the Peace
Convention at Washington.   The reference to his
course there, in the first of these sketches, renders it
unnecessary to say more at present.   Eminent statesmen, now in high position in the national councils, can
testify to his zealous and unremitting labors in that
Convention to preserve and perpetuate the union of
the States ; and none, doubtless, will do so more cor-
dially than the venerable military chieftain* who, sixty
years ago, was his friend and fellow-student in the
office of an eminent lawyer in Petersburgh.

Judge Ruffin returned home, dispirited and discour-
aged by the temper displayed in the Convention, and
still more by the proceedings of Congress.   He still
cherished hopes of reconciliation, however, when, without any canvass by or for him, he was elected to the
Convention which, on the twentieth of May, 1861,
adopted, by a unanimous vote, the Ordinance of Secession.

Having given that vote, he was not the man to
shrink from the responsibilities it involved.   In common with every other respectable citizen in the State,
he felt it his duty to encourage and animate our soldiers, and to contribute liberally to their support and
that of their families at home.   His sons who were
able to bear arms were in the battle-field, and his
family endured all the privations, and practiced all
the self-denial common to our people ; cheerfully dis-
pensing with the luxuries of life, and laboring assidu-

* General Winfield Scott.

ously for the relief of the army and the needy around them.

Toward this most eminent and venerable citizen, whose name added weight to the dignity and influence of the whole country, what was the policy of Major-General Couch, encamped on his grounds, in the pleasant month of May? The plantation had already suffered from the depredations of Major - General Wheeler's cavalry of the Confederate army in its hurried transit; but it was reserved for General Couch to give it the finishing touch. In a few words, ten miles of fencing were burned up, from one end of it to the other; not an ear of corn, not a sheaf of wheat, not a bundle of fodder was left; the army wagons were driven into the cultivated fields and orchards and meadows, and fires were made under the fruit-trees; the sheep and hogs were shot down and left to rot on the ground, and several thousand horses and cattle were turned in on the wheat crops, then just heading. All the horses, seventeen in number, were carried off, and all the stock. An application for protection, and remonstrance against wanton damage, were met with indifference and contempt.

Such being the course of one of General Sherman's subaltern officers in time of peace, it is natural to turn to General Sherman himself, and inquire what was the example set by him in the progress of "the great march." He speaks for himself, and history will yet deliver an impartial verdict on such a summing up:

"We consumed the corn and fodder in the region of country thirty miles on either side of a line from

Atlanta to Savannah; also the sweet potatoes, hogs, sheep, and poultry, and carried off more than ten thousand horses and mules. I estimate the damage done to the State of Georgia at one hundred million dollars; at least twenty million dollars of which inured to our advantage, and the remainder was simple waste and destruction." (Official Report.)

Simple people, who understand nothing of military necessities, must be permitted to stand aghast at such a recital, and ask why was this? To what end? What far-sighted policy dictated such wholesale havoc? Lord Cornwallis—a foreigner—acting as a representative of the *mother* country, seeking to reclaim her alienated children, we have seen everywhere anxious to conciliate, generously active to spare the country as much as possible, to preserve it for the interests of the mother country, and enforcing strict discipline in his army for the benefit of the service. What changes have been effected in the *morale* of war by nearly a century of Christian progress and civilization since Lord Cornwallis's day? An army, in the middle of the nineteenth century, acting as the representative of *sister States*, seeking to reclaim " wayward sisters "— an army enlisted with the most extraordinary and emphatic avowals of purely philanthropic motives that the world has ever heard—an army marching through what it professes to consider AS ITS OWN COUNTRY—this army leaves a waste and burning track behind it of sixty miles' width!

> " O bloodiest picture in the book of Time !
> Sarmatia fell unwept, without a crime ;

> Found not a generous friend, a pitying foe,
> Strength in her arms, nor mercy in her woe!
> Dropped from her nerveless grasp the shattered spear,
> Closed her bright eye, and curbed her high career."

The gay and airy pen-and-ink sketches, furnished to the Northern press by "our own army correspondents," of the exploits of bummers, the jocular descriptions of treasure-seekers, the triumphant records of fire, famine, and slaughter, served up with elegant illustrations—wood-cuts in Harper's best style—and, if likely to be a trifle too glaring for even radical sensibilities, toned down and made to assume an air of retributive justice by a timely allusion to the "wretched slaves"— these interesting reports, piquant and gayly-colored and suggestive though they were, were yet dull and tame and faded in comparison with the dismal reality. And all this "waste and destruction," it will be the verdict of posterity, even the calmed sense of the present generation will agree, was wholly uncalled for, wholly unnecessary, contributed in no way to the prosperous and speedy termination of the war, but added materially to the losses by the war of the General Government, lit up the fires of hatred in many a hitherto loyal Southern breast, brutalized and demoralized the whole Federal army, and was in short inexcusable in every aspect except upon the determination to exterminate the Southern people. We knew that there were men in the Church and in the State who openly avowed such aspirations; but as to the great body of the sober, intelligent, and conscientious Northern people, we do them the justice to believe

that when the history of the war *at the South* comes
to be truthfully written, they will receive its records
with incredulity; and when belief is compelled, will
turn from them shuddering.

The smoke of burning Columbia, and of the fair
villages and countless plantations that lay in the route,
where, for hundreds of miles, many a house was left
blazing, and not a panel of fence was to be seen, rolled
slowly up our sky; and panic-stricken refugees, homeless and penniless, brought every day fresh tales of
havoc and ruin. By the eleventh of March, General
Sherman was in possession of Fayetteville, in our own
State.

The coïncidences in the plan, and the contrasts in
the mode of conducting the campaigns of Lord Cornwallis and General Sherman, are striking, and suggestive to the student of history. Cornwallis hesitated
whether to strike North-Carolina in the heart of the
whig settlements—between the Yadkin and the Catawba—or enter among his friends between the Pedee
and Cape Fear, and ultimately decided to accomplish
both purposes. In January, 1781, Sir James Henry
Craig captured Wilmington, and on the nineteenth of
February, Lord Cornwallis forced the passage of the
Catawba at Beattie's Ford. General Schofield had
possession of Wilmington when General Sherman,
making *a feint* at Charlotte, captured Fayetteville.

In Lord Cornwallis's progress through Carolina he
met with every thing to exasperate him in the conduct
of the people. On his first entrance into Charlotte,
September, 1780, the whole British army was actually

held at bay for half an hour by a body of about one hundred and fifty militia, and a few volunteers, commanded by Major Joseph Graham, posted behind the court-house and houses, and commanded by Colonel Davie, who was "determined to give his lordship an earnest of what he might expect in the State." Three separate charges of the British Legion were repulsed by this handful of devoted men, who retired at last on being flanked by the infantry, in perfect order, with but a loss of eleven killed and wounded, while the British admitted a loss of forty-three killed and wounded. "When the Legion was afterward reproached for cowardice in suffering such a check from so small a detail of militia, they excused themselves by saying that the confidence with which the Americans behaved made them apprehend an ambuscade, for surely nothing of that sort was to be expected in an open village at mid-day." I have by me as I write, in Colonel Davie's own handwriting, his account of "the affair at Charlotte," as he modestly styles it, and it is well worth comparing with Tarleton's and Stedman's report of the same. A more brilliant and audacious exploit was not performed during the whole Revolutionary war. A series of such annoyances, heading and dogging the British army at every step all through that country, gained for Charlotte the well-earned and enviable *sobriquet* of "The Hornets' Nest," and the commander-in-chief paid the whole region the compliment of declaring that "Mecklenburg and Rowan were the two most rebellious counties in America."

Yet Cornwallis burned no houses here—plundered

no plantations. His aim was very apparently to conciliate if possible, to teach the people to look to him
for protection and a good government. To be sure,
he had not enjoyed the benefit of a West-Point military training—he was evidently in profound ignorance
of the advantages to be derived from the principle of
" smashing things generally," as he passed along; but
he was, nevertheless, (perhaps in consequence,) a *gentleman*, and an accomplished statesman, as well as a
consummate soldier. He well knew—

> " —— who overcomes
> By force, hath overcome but half his foe."

As to Fayetteville, and her lot in these later days,
no such slight sketch as this will suffice for the story.
Perhaps no town in the South had surpassed her in
the ardor and liberality with which (after secession
had become the law of the State) she supported the
war. She gave her bravest sons; her best blood was
poured out like water in the cause of the South, and
then she gave of her substance. The grace of giving
had surely been bestowed upon the people of Cumberland without measure, for there seemed literally
no end to their liberality. For four years the columns
of their papers had exhibited an almost weekly list of
donations, that in number and value would have done
infinite credit to a much wealthier community. The
ladies, as usual, were especially active and indefatigable. Where, indeed, in all the sunny South were they
not? And why should they not have been? They
were working for their fathers, husbands, sons, bro-

thers, and lovers, and for principles which these beloved ones had instructed them to cherish. Would it
not have been culpable in the last degree for the women of the country to have remained even indifferent
to a cause (good or bad) for which the men were laying
down their lives ? Why should they not take joyfully
all privations and all hardships, for the sake of these,
and soothe the agony of bereavement with the belief
that they who needed their cares no longer, lying
rolled in their bloody blankets in the bosom of Virginia, or on the fatal hills of Pennsylvania, had died
in a good cause and were resting in honored graves ?
Who shall question the course of the women of the
South in this war, or dare to undervalue their lofty
heroism and fortitude, unsurpassed in story or in song ?
When I forget you, O ye daughters of my country !
your labors of love, your charity, faith, and patience,
all through the dark and bloody day, lighting up the
gloom of war with the tender graces of woman's devotion and self-denial, and now, in even darker hours,
your energy and cheerful submission in toil and poverty and humiliation—when I cease to do homage to
your virtues, and to your excellences, may my right
hand forget its cunning and my voice be silent in the
dust !

The people of Fayetteville supported the Confederate Government warmly to the last gasp, upon the
principle that *united*, the South might stand—*divided*,
she certainly would fall. After the failure of the
Peace Commission, the citizens met and passed vigorous war resolutions, calling on all classes to rally once

more in self-defense—a proceeding which did more credit to their zeal than to their ability to read the signs of the times ; for, rally or no rally, the fate of the Confederacy was already written on the wall.

All these antecedents doubtless conspired to give Fayetteville a bad character in the opinion of our Northern brethren, who, for their part, were bent on peace-making ; and accordingly, when the hour and the man arrived, on the eleventh of March, 1865, she found she must pay the penalty. A skirmish took place in the streets between General Sherman's advanced-guard and a part of General Hampton's cavalry, which covered the retreat of Hardee's division across the Cape Fear. This, no doubt, increased the exasperation of feeling toward this " nest of rebels," and the determination to put a check to all future operations there in behalf of the cause.   In less than two hours after the entrance of the Federal forces, so adroitly had every house in the town and its suburbs been ransacked and plundered, that it may be doubted if all Fayetteville, the next day, could have contributed two whole shirts or a bushel of meal to the relief of the Confederate army.   The incidents of that most memorable day, and for several days succeeding, would fill (and *will* fill) a volume; and as for the nights, they were illuminated by the glare of blazing houses all through the pine groves for several miles around Fayetteville.   One of the first of the " soldiers in blue " who entered the town, accosted in the street a most distinguished and venerable clergyman, Rev. William Hooper, D.D., LL.D., more than seventy years of age

—the grandson of one of the signers of the Declaration of Independence—and who had suffered reproach for his adherence to the Union, and whose very appearance should have challenged respect and deference—accosted him as a " d—d rebel," and putting a pistol to his head, demanded and carried off his watch and purse.

Southerners can not write calmly of such scenes yet. Their houses were turned into seraglios, every portable article of value, plate, china and glass-ware, provisions and books were carried off, and the remainder destroyed; hundreds of carriages and vehicles of all kinds were burned in piles; where houses were isolated they were burned; women were grossly insulted, and robbed of clothing and jewelry; nor were darker and nameless tragedies wanting in lonely situations. No; they hardly dare trust themselves to think of these things. "That way lies madness." But the true story of "THE GREAT MARCH" will yet be written.

Not the least remarkable of all these noble strategical operations was the fact that black and white suffered alike. Nothing more strikingly evinces the entire demoralization and want of honor that prevailed. The negro whom they came to liberate they afterward plundered; his cabin was stripped of his little valuables, as well as his master's house of its luxuries; his humble silver watch was seized, as well as the gentleman's gold repeater. This policy is also modern, and due to the enlightenment of the nineteenth century. A good many years ago, a grand liberation of slaves took place, where the leaders and deliverer sanctioned the " spoiling of the Egyptians," but they hardly picked the pockets of the freedmen afterward.

During the month of March our central counties were traversed by straggling bodies of Confederate soldiers, fragments of the once powerful army of Tennessee, hurrying down toward Raleigh to concentrate under General Johnston once more, in the vain hope of being able yet to effect something. Tennesseeans, Texans, Georgians, Alabamians, men who had been in every fight in the West, from Corinth to Perrysville, from Perrysville to Atlanta—men who had left pleasant homes, wives and children, many of whom they knew were without a house to shelter them;

"For the blackness of ashes marked where it stood,
    And a wild mother's scream o'er her famishing brood!"

The whole population of our town poured out to see these war-worn men; to cheer them; to feed and shelter them. The little children gathered handfuls of the early daffodils "that take the winds of March with beauty," and flung to them. What we had to eat we gave them, day after day. Repeatedly the whole of a family dinner was taken from the table and carried out to the street, the children joyfully assisting. They were our soldiers—our own brave boys. The cause was desperate, we knew—the war was nearly over—our delusions were at an end; but while we had it, our last loaf to our soldiers—a cheer, and a blessing, with dim eyes, as they rode away.

CHAPTER IV.

IN the preceding chapter, attention was drawn to
the striking contrast between the policy pursued by
General Sherman toward the inhabitants of the country
he was invading, and that of his illustrious predecessor
in the days of the Revolution. I think there can be
but little doubt as to which of these distinguished
commanders is entitled to most credit on the score of
humanity. General Sherman's friends, considering
that he who conducts a campaign to a successful issue
may well afford to disregard the means to the desired
end, will doubtless support his policy; for where
Cornwallis failed, he succeeded, and succeeded bril-
liantly. Lord Cornwallis, however, in the general be-
nevolence of his character—tempering, as far as was
practicable, the severities of war with forbearance and
generosity—is more justly entitled to stand by the
side of WASHINGTON than any other military commander of his age. As to his failure, time has shown
that it was well for both countries that he did fail;
and his memory is crowned with more unfading laurels

than the title of mere conqueror could have conferred. Self-control, discipline, and magnanimous consideration for the weak and the defenseless are better than burning houses and a devastated country.

If, however, it still be asserted that humanity is *necessarily* no part of a soldier's duty, and that his business is to win the fight, no matter how, an appeal to the authorities on such points, recognized in all civilized nations, will show that the law is otherwise laid down.

General Sherman begins his famous letter to General Hampton with the assertion that "the right to forage is older than history." What was the precise character of this right among barbarians in the morning twilight of civilization it may hardly be worth our while to inquire. But we have clear historic evidence that, long before the coming of the Prince of Peace, in the earliest ages of profane history, among civilized nations the "right to forage" did *not* mean a right to indiscriminate pillage, "waste, and destruction"—destruction extending not only to the carrying off of the cattle necessary in farming operations, but to the agricultural tools and implements of every description. More than twenty centuries ago, Xenophon, at the head of the Ten Thousand, accomplished his famous retreat from Babylon to the sea. The incidents of that great march are given by himself in a narrative, whose modesty, spirit, and elegance have charmed all subsequent ages. His views as to the right to forage are clearly stated in the following passage, taken from *Kent's Commentaries on International Law* — an authority that was studied by General Sherman at West-Point, and was taught by him when Superintendent of the Military Academy of Louisiana. Treating of plunder on land, depredations upon private property, etc., he says:

"Such conduct has been condemned in all ages by the wise and virtuous, and it is usually punished severely by those commanders of disciplined troops who have studied war as a science, and are animated by a sense of duty or the love of fame. We may infer the opinion of Xenophon on this subject, (and he was a warrior as well as a philosopher,) when he states, in the *Cyropœdia*, that Cyrus of Persia gave orders to his army, *when marching upon the enemy's borders*, not to disturb the cultivators of the soil; and there have been such ordinances in modern times for the protection of innocent and pacific pursuits. If the conqueror goes beyond these limits wantonly, or when it is not clearly indispensable to the just purposes of war, and seizes private property of pacific persons for the sake of gain, and destroys private dwellings, or public edifices devoted to civil purposes only; or makes war upon monuments of art, and models of taste, he violates the modern usages of war, and is sure to meet with indignant resentment, and to be held up to the general scorn and detestation of the world." (Part I. Sec. 5.)

To this authority may be added a still more modern and binding exposition of the laws of war. *Halleck's International Law and Laws of War*, written and published in 1861 by an officer of the Government, and for a time a major-general and commander-in-chief of the Federal army, may be considered as the latest and ablest summary of the best authorities on these subjects. It was in the hands of General Sherman and his officers, and its decisions may be regarded as final. Nothing can be more explicit or more emphatic than the following extracts. First, as to general right of war in an enemy's property (on land) :

" The general theory of war is, as heretofore stated, that all private property may be taken by the conqueror; and such was the ancient practice. But the modern usage is, not to touch private property on land without making compensation, except in certain specified cases. These exceptions may be stated under three general heads : 1st. Confiscations or seizures by way of penalty for military offenses ; 2d. Forced contributions for the support of the invading army, or as an indemnity for the expenses of maintaining order, and affording protection to the conquered inhabitants ; and 3d. Property taken on the field of battle, or in storming a fortress or town.

" In the first place, we may seize upon private property, by way of penalty for the illegal acts of individuals, or of the community to which they belong. Thus, if an individual be guilty of conduct in violation of the laws of war, we may seize and confiscate the private property of the offender.   So, also, if the offense attach itself to a particular community or town, all the individuals of that community or town are liable to punishment ; and we may seize upon their property, or levy upon them a retaliatory contribution by way of penalty. When, however, we can discover and secure the individuals so offending, it is more just to inflict the punishment on them only; but it is a general law of war that communities are accountable for the acts of their individual members. If these individuals are not given up, or can not be discovered, it is usual to impose a contribution upon the civil authorities of the place where the offense is committed; and these authorities raise the amount of the contribution by a tax levied on their constituents." (Chap. 19, pages 457, 458.)

If the town of Fayetteville had in any way become peculiarly obnoxious to the Federal army, one would have thought that a glance into Halleck might have satisfied the commanding officers as to their rights and duties there on the eleventh of March, 1865. Not a word here of plunder, pillage, or arson. There can be no doubt that Fayetteville would have gladly compounded for her offenses by a tax of almost any possible amount, levied and collected in a lawful and civilized way, in preference to her actual experiences.

Next, as to right of forage, etc.:

"In the second place, we have a *right* to make the enemy's country contribute to the expenses of the war. Troops in the enemy's country may be subsisted either by regular magazines, by forced requisitions, or by authorized pillage. It is not always politic, or even possible, to provide regular magazines for the entire supply of an army during the active operations of a campaign. When this can not be done, the general is obliged either to resort to military requisitions, or to intrust their subsistence to the troops themselves. The inevitable consequences of the latter system are universal pillage, and a total relaxation of discipline : the loss of private property, and the violation of individual rights, are usually followed by the massacre of straggling parties; and the *ordinary peaceful and non-combatant inhabitants are converted into bitter and implacable enemies.* The system is, therefore, regarded as both impolitic and unjust, and is coming into general disuse among the more civilized nations —at least for the support of the main army. In case of small detachments, where great rapidity of motion is requisite, it sometimes becomes necessary for the troops to procure their subsistence wherever they can. In such a case, the seizure of private property becomes a necessary consequence of the military operations, and is, therefore, unavoidable. Other cases of similar character might be mentioned. But even in most of these special and extreme cases, provisions might be made for subsequently compensating the owners for the loss of their property." (Page 459.)

" The evils resulting from irregular requisitions, and foraging for the ordinary supplies of an army, are so very great, and so generally admitted, that it has become a recognized maxim of war, that the commanding officer who permits indiscriminate pillage, and allows the taking of private property without a strict accountability, whether he be engaged in defensive or offensive operations, fails in his duty to his own government, and violates the usages of modern warfare. It is sometimes alleged, in excuse for such conduct, that the general is unable to restrain his troops; but in the eye of the law there is no excuse; for *he who can not preserve order in his army has no right to command it.* In collecting military contributions, trustworthy troops should be sent with the foragers, to prevent them from engaging in irregular and unauthorized pillage; and the party should always be accompanied by officers of the staff and administrative corps, to see to the proper execution of the orders, and to report any irregularities on the part of the troops. In case any corps should engage in unauthorized pillage, due restitution should be made to the inhabitants, and the expenses of such restitution deducted from the pay and allowances of the corps by which such excess is committed. But modify and restrict it as you will, the system of subsisting armies on the private property of an enemy's subjects without compensation is very objectionable, and almost inevitably leads to cruel and disastrous results. There is, therefore, very seldom a sufficient reason for resorting to it." (Chap. 19, page 451.)

"While there is some uncertainty as to the exact limit fixed by the voluntary law of nations to our right to appropriate to our own use the property of an enemy, or to subject it to military contributions, *there is no doubt whatever respecting its waste and useless destruction. This is forbidden alike by the law of nature and the rules of war.* There are numerous instances in military history where whole districts of country have been totally ravaged and laid waste. Such operations have sometimes been defended on the ground of necessity, or as a means of preventing greater evils. 'Such violent remedies,' says Vattel, 'are to be sparingly applied: there must be reasons of suitable importance to justify the use of them. He who does the like in an enemy's country when impelled by no necessity, or induced by feeble reasons, becomes the scourge of mankind.'

"The general rule by which we should regulate our conduct toward an enemy is *that of moderation ; and on no occasion should we unnecessarily destroy his property*. 'The pillage and destruction of towns,' says Vattel, 'the devastation of the open country, ravaging and setting fire to houses, are measures no less odious and detestable on every occasion when they are evidently put in practice without absolute necessity, or at least very cogent reasons. But as the perpetrators of such outrageous deeds might attempt to palliate them, under pretext of deservedly punishing the enemy, be it here observed that the natural and voluntary law of nations does not allow us to inflict such punishments, except for enormous offenses against the law of nations; and even then it is glorious to listen to the voice of humanity and clemency, when rigor is not absolutely necessary.' " (Pages 455 –456.)

To these unimpeachable decisions I can not refrain from adding that of President Woolsey, of Yale College. In his Introduction to the Study of International Law, sec. 130, pp. 304–5, he says: " The property, movable and immovable, of private persons in an invaded country is to remain uninjured. But if the wants of the hostile army require, it may be taken by authorized persons at a fair value; but marauding must be checked by discipline and penalties." And even as to "permissible requisitions," which Wellington regarded as iniquitous, and opposed as "*likely to injure those who resorted to them*," President Woolsey adds that they "are demoralizing; they arouse the avarice of officers, and *leave a sting in the memory of oppressed nations.*"

It is this *sting*, left in the breasts of the Southern people, these bitter hatreds aroused by the indiscriminate and licensed pillage to which they were subjected, which are more to be deprecated than any consequence of the blood shed in fair and open fight during the war. Hard blows do not necessarily make bad blood between generous foes. It is the ungenerous policy of the exulting conqueror that adds poison to the bleeding wounds.

From a mass of agreeing testimony, as to the conduct of the Federal troops on their entrance into our State, I select the following letter from a clergyman of distinction, the authorized head of one of the most influential denominations in the State; a man of national reputation for the learning, ability, and piety with which he adorns his high office in the Church of God. Let it be carefully read, and its calm and moderate tone be fairly estimated and appreciated:

.   .   .   .   "I am altogether indisposed to obtrude myself on the public, and especially to bring before it complaints of personal grievance; but it seemed to me important, not only for the interests of justice, but of humanity, that the truth should be declared concerning the mode in which the late civil war was carried on, and I did not see that I was exempted from this duty rather than any one else who had personal knowledge of facts bearing on that subject. For this reason I made the statement to my Convention which you allude to, and for the same reason I have, after some hesitation, felt bound to give you the information you ask.

"When General Sherman was moving on Cheraw, in South-Carolina, one corps of his army, under General Slocum, I believe, advanced in a parallel line north of him, and extended into this State. Some companies of Kilpatrick's cavalry attached to this corps came on Friday, third March, to Wadesboro, in Anson county, where I was then residing. As their approach was known, many persons thought it best to withdraw from the place before the cavalry entered it; but I determined to remain, as I could not remove my family, and I did not suppose that I would suffer any serious injury. I saw the troops galloping in, and sat down quietly to my books, reading, having asked the other members of my family to remain in a room in the rear of the building. After a time a soldier knocked at the door, which I opened. He at once, with many oaths, demanded my watch, which I refused to give him. He then drew a pistol and presented it at me, and threatened to shoot me immediately if I did not surrender it. I still refused, and, the altercation becoming loud, my wife heard it, ran into the room and earnestly besought me to give it up, which I then did. Having secured this, he demanded money, but as we had none but Confederate, he would not take that. He then proceeded to rifle our trunks and drawers, took some of my clothes from these, and my wife's jewelry; but he would have nothing to do with heavy articles as, fortunately, he had no means of carrying them off. He then left the house, and I went in search of his officers to ask them to compel him to return what he had taken from me. This might seem a hopeless effort; for the same game had been played in every house in the town where there seemed to be any thing worth taking. However, in my case, the officers promised, if I could identify the robber, to compel him to make restitution. The men, accordingly, were drawn up in line, and their commander and I went along it examining their countenances, but my acquaintance was not among them. It turned out that he had gone from my house to that of a neighbor, to carry on the same work, and during my absence had returned to my house, taken a horse from the stable, and then moved off to his camp at some miles' distance. The next day other bands visited us, taking groceries from us and demanding watches and money. They broke open the storehouses in the village; and as at one of these I had some tierces of china and boxes of books, these they knocked to pieces, breaking the china, of course, and scattering the books, but not carrying them off, as they probably did not much value them, and had, fortunately, no wagons. I finally recovered nearly all of them. Another part of Sherman's army,

in their march through Richmond county, passed by
two railroad stations where I had a piano and other
furniture, which they destroyed ; and also at Fayetteville I had furniture at the house of a friend, which
shared the fate of his. Yet I was among those who
suffered *comparatively lightly.* Where the army went
with its wagons, they swept the country of almost
every thing of value that was portable. In some instances defenseless men were killed for plunder. A
Mr. James C. Bennet, one of the oldest and wealthiest
men in Anson county, was shot at the door of his own
house because he did not give up his watch and money,
which had been previously taken from him by another
party.

"These and the like atrocities ought to be known ;
for even men who do not much fear the judgments of
God, are kept somewhat in awe by the apprehension
of the sentence of the civilized world and of posterity.

"In conclusion, I must say that I wish as little reference to be made to me, and the injuries done me, as
is consistent with the faithful narrative which you
have undertaken to give of the last ninety days of the
war in North-Carolina.

"I remain, very truly and respectfully yours,
                    "THOMAS ATKINSON."

Bishop Atkinson, it is well known, was the first to
set the example, after the war was closed, of leading
his church half-way to reünite the church connection
North and South. An example of Christian charity,
meekness, and forbearance most worthy of our admiration and imitation.

CHAPTER V.

WHEN Lord Cornwallis was on his march to Wil-.
mington, after the battle of Guilford Court-House,
passing by the residence of a planter near Cross Creek,
(now Fayetteville,) the army halted. The young mis-
tress of the mansion, a gay and very beautiful matron
of eighteen, with the impulsive curiosity of a child,
ran to her front piazza to gaze at the pageant. Some
officers dismounting approached the house. She addressed one of the foremost, and begged that he would
point out to her Lord Cornwallis, if he was there, for
" she wished to see a lord." "Madam," said the gentleman, removing his hat, "I am Lord Cornwallis."
Then with the formal courtesy of the day he led her
into the house, giving to the frightened family every
assurance of protection. With the high breeding of a
gentleman and the frankness of a soldier, he won all.

hearts during his stay, from the venerable grandmother in her chair to the gay girl who had first accosted him. While the army remained, not an article was disturbed on the plantation, though, as he himself warned them, there were stragglers in his wake whom he could not detect, and who failed not to do what mischief they could in the way of plundering, after he had passed. 'Tis eighty-four years ago, and that blooming girl's granddaughters tell the story with grateful regard for the memory of the noble Englishman, who never forgot what was due to a defenseless homestead, and who well deserves to be held in admiration by woman.*

How tender the light that plays round this great captain's memory ! Smarting from recent virtual defeat, hurrying through a hostile country, disappointed in his expectations of receiving relief and reënforcement in this very neighborhood of Cross Creek, he is master of himself and of his army through all reverses of fortune—gentle and considerate in the midst of adversity.

The recollections of that young Southern matron's grandson, Charles B. Mallett, Esq., of the great army passing so lately over the very same ground, and of their visit to his plantation, afford matter for curious consideration and comparison. These are his reminiscences :

" The china and glass-ware were all carried out of

* His own beloved young wife, dying of a broken heart on the separation caused by his coming to America, " directed on her death-bed that a thorn-tree should be planted on her grave, as nearly as possible over her heart, significant

the house by the Federal soldiers, and deliberately smashed in the yard. The furniture—piano, beds, tables, bureaus—were all cut to pieces with axes; the pantries and smoke-houses were stripped of their contents; the negro houses were all plundered; the poultry, cows, horses, etc., were shot down and carried off; and then, after all this, the houses were all fired and burned to the ground. The cotton factory belonging to the family was also burned, as were six others in the neighborhood of Fayetteville."

I have also the statement of a near neighbor of this gentleman, John M. Rose, Esq., condensed as follows:

" The Federal soldiers searched my house from garret to cellar, and plundered it of every thing portable; took all my provisions, emptied the pantries of all stores, and did not leave me a mouthful of any kind of supplies for one meal's victuals. They took all my clothing, even the hat off my head, and the shoes and pants from my person; took most of my wife's and children's clothing, all of our bedding; destroyed my furniture, and robbed all my negroes. At leaving they set fire to my fences, out-houses, and dwelling, which, fortunately, I was able to extinguish. The remains of a dozen slaughtered cattle were left in my yard. (Nine dwellings were burned to the ground in this neighborhood. Four gentlemen, whose names are given, were hung up by the neck till nearly dead, to force them to tell where valuables were hidden. One

of the sorrow that destroyed her life. Her request was complied with, and that thorn-tree is still living," (1857.)—The Cornwallis Correspondence, chap. 1. p. 14.

was shot in his own house, and died soon after.) The
yard and lot were searched, and all my money, and
that of several companies which I represent, was found
and taken. All my stocks and bonds were likewise
carried off. My wagon, and garden, and lot implements were all burned in my yard. The property
taken from another family—the jewelry, plate, money,
etc.—was estimated to be worth not less than twenty-
five thousand dollars. Hundreds of pleasure vehicles
in the town were either wantonly burned in parcels
and separately, or carried off with the army. Houses
in the suburbs and vicinity suffered more severely than
those in the town. No private dwellings in the town
were burned, and after the guards were placed the
pillage ceased. The misfortune was, that the guards
were not placed till the houses had been sacked."

I have other statements, but perhaps these are sufficient for my present purpose.* I have given none that
can not be verified if necessary, though they differ
widely from those of a book lately published at the
North, entitled The Story of the Great March, and
which is doubtless regarded there as of unquestionable
authority. On page 251 I observe it is stated, "Private property in Fayetteville has been respected to a
degree which is remarkable;" and on page 253: " The

---

* The writer might have mentioned that J. P. McLean was hung up by the neck
three times and shot at once, to make him disclose hidden valuables. W. T. Horne,
Jesse Hawley, and Alexander McAuthor, were all hung up until nearly dead. John
Waddill was shot down and killed in his own house. The country residences of
C. T. Haigh, J. C. Haigh, Archibald Graham, and W. T. Horne, were all burned
within a short distance of one another; this was all in one neighborhood. Dr.
Hicks, of Duplin, was hung until nearly dead, and will probably never recover.
So it was elsewhere.—EDITOR.

city of Fayetteville was offensively rebellious, and it
has been a matter of surprise that our soldiers, who
are quick to understand the distinction, have not made
the citizens feel it in one way or another." It is just
possible that Major Nichols did not know the truth;
that, being very evidently of an easy and credulous
temper, and too busy- making up his little book for
sale, he allowed himself to be imposed upon by wicked
jokers. Let us all believe that he knew nothing of
the robberies that were going on. He was evidently
hard of hearing, besides; for he says, page 240, " I
have yet to hear of a single outrage offered to a woman by a soldier of our army." Let us all believe
that he was too deeply interested in his interviews
with the handsome " quadroon family," mentioned on
page 237, to know what was going on among the
whites. By the way, it would seem these quadroon
girls were too deep for him too. His reported conversation with the family is a very amusing tissue of
blunders and misrepresentation. Foot-notes should
certainly accompany the thirtieth edition, and in particular it should be stated of these " intelligent quadroons," not one of whom was ever named Hannah, and
not one of any name was ever sold, that not one of
them has yet left the lot of their old master, or expressed a wish to leave. Major Nichols does not
seem to know much; but he probably knows this,
that it was not for want of asking that these handsome quadroons did not go.

Enough of such disclosures and of such scenes. If
it be asked why these have been presented, and why

I seek to prolong these painful memories, and to keep alive the remembrances that ought rather to slumber and be forgotten with the dead past, let me reply that it is deliberately, and of set purpose, that I sketch these outlines of a great tragedy for our Northern friends to ponder. The South has suffered; that they admit in general terms, and add, "*Such is war.*" I desire to call their attention to the fact that such is NOT war, as their own standards declare; that the career of the grand army in the Great March, brilliant as was the design, masterly as was the execution, and triumphant as was the issue, is yet, in its details, a story of which they have no reason to be proud, and which, when truly told, if there be one spark of generosity, one drop of the milk of human kindness in Northern breasts, should turn their bitterness toward the South into tender pity, their exultation over her into a manly regret and remorse. They do not know— they never will know unless Southerners themselves shall tell the mournful story—what the sword hath done in her fair fields and her pleasant places. Their triumphant stories and war-lyrics are not faithful expositors of the woe and ruin wrought upon a defenseless people. When the sounds of conflict have finally died away, I would fain see the calmed senses of a great people who, having fairly won the fight, can afford to be magnanimous, take in clearly the situation of the whole Southern country, and "repent them for their brother Benjamin, and come to the house of God, and weep sore for their brother, and say, O Lord God, why is this come to pass that there should be to-day one tribe lacking in Israel?"

Thousands of delicate women, bred up in affluence, are now bravely working· with their hands for their daily bread ; many in old age, and alone in the world, are bereft of all their earthly possessions.   Thousands of families are absolutely penniless, who have never before known a want ungratified.   Let me not be mistaken to represent Southerners as shrinking from work, or ignobly bewailing the loss of luxury and ease. The dignity and the " perennial nobleness" of labor. were never more fairly asserted than among us now, and I have never seen, or read, or heard of a braver acceptance of the situation, a more cheerful submission to God's will, or a more spirited application to unaccustomed toils and duties, than are exhibited here this day.   Nobody is ashamed of himself, or ashamed of his position, or of his necessities.   What the South wants is not charity—charity as an alms—but generosity ; that generosity which forbears reproach, or insult, or gay and clamorous exultation, but which silently clears the way of all difficulties, and lends an arm to a fainting, wounded brother; that says, "There *must* be an inheritance for them that be escaped of Benjamin."

It is for this that I present these sketches, which, but for some good to be accomplished by them, would better have never been written.   Where wrongs can not be redressed, or their recital be made available for good, they would far better be buried in oblivion; the wrong-doer and the sufferer alike awaiting in dread repose the final award of the Great Tribunal.

How shall the South begin her new life ?   How,

disfranchised and denied her civil rights, shall she start the wheels of enterprise and business that shall bring work and bread to her plundered, penniless people? How shall her widows and orphans be fed, her schools and colleges be supported, her churches be maintained, unless her rights and liberties be regained—unless every effort be made to give her wounds repose, and restore health and energy to her paralyzed and shattered frame? Is there any precedent in history of a war that ended with the freeing not only from all obligation to labor, but from all disposition to labor, of all the operatives of the conquered country? Is not the social status of the South at present without a parallel? Just emerging from an exhausting and devastating war, the country might well be crippled and poverty-stricken; but with three or four millions of enfranchised slaves, a population that is even now hastening to inaugurate the worst evils of insubordination, idleness, and pauperism among us, what hope for us unless the Northern sense of justice can be aroused into speedy action!

While General Sherman's wagons were wallowing in the mud between Fayetteville and Goldsboro, vain attempts were being made in Raleigh to galvanize into some show of action and strength the fragments of an army that were concentrating there. General Lee's desperate situation in Virginia was not understood and realized by the multitude, nor that the Confederate territory was fast narrowing down to the northern counties of Central North-Carolina, and that Raleigh was the last capital city we could claim. Beau-

regard, Johnston, Hardee, Hoke, Hampton, Wheeler—
names that had thrilled the whole Southern country
with pride and exultation—they were all there, and
for a time people endeavored to believe that Raleigh
might be defended. General Sherman's plans appeared
to be inscrutable. When he left Columbia, Charlotte
was supposed to be his aim; but when he fell suddenly upon Fayetteville, then Raleigh was to be his next
stage. The astute plan of a junction with Schofield
at Goldsboro, which appears now to have been pre-
arranged while he was yet in Savannah, did not dawn
upon our minds till it was too late to prevent it. The
fight at Bentonsville was a desperate and vain attempt
to do what might possibly have been done before, and
in that last wild struggle many a precious life was
given in vain. With sad anxiety for the fate of those
we loved, with sinking hearts, we heard, from day to
day, from Averasboro and from Bentonsville, of the wild
charge, the short, fierce struggle, and the inevitable
retreat, little thinking that these were indeed the last
life-throbs of our dying cause.

There was one from our own circle, whose story is
but a representative one of the many thousand such
that now darken what was once the Sunny South.
He had joined the army in the beginning of the war,
and his wife and children had fled from their pleasant
home near New-Berne, on its first occupation by the
Federal forces, leaving the negroes, plantation, house,
furniture, and all to the invaders. They had taken
refuge at Chapel Hill among old friends; and in a poor
and inconvenient home, those who had counted their

wealth by thousands were glad of a temporary shelter, as was the case with hundreds of families from the east, scattered all over the central part of the State. The energetic wife laid aside the habits of a lifetime and went to work, while her brave husband was in the army.   From New-Berne to Richmond, from Charleston to the Blackwater, we, who had known him from boyhood, traced his gallant career, sharing his wife's triumphs in his successes, and her fears in his perils.   Her health in unaccustomed toils began to fail, but we looked forward hopefully to the time when she might return to her beautiful home on the sea-shore, where a blander air would restore her.   So we read his loving, cheerful letters, and believed that the life which had been spared through so many battles would yet be guarded for the sake of the wife and the curly-haired little ones.   On the twenty-second of March, riding unguardedly near a thicket, our friend received the fire of a squad of sharp-shooters concealed there.   He fell from his horse and was carried to a place of safety, where he lay on the muddy ground of the trampled battle-field for a few hours, murmuring faintly at intervals, "My wife! my poor wife!" till death mercifully came.   He was wrapped by his faithful servant in his blood-stained uniform and muddy blankets as he lay ; a coarse box was procured with great difficulty, and so the soldier was brought back to his family. His last visit home had been just before the fall of Fort Fisher ; and when the news of the attack came, though his furlough was not out by ten days, yet he left at once for Wilmington, saying, "It was every man's duty to be at the front." He had returned to us now, " off duty forever." Loving hands laid him slowly and sadly down to a soldier's honored rest, while his little children stood around the grave. The wife made an effort to live for these children. She bore up through that woful spring and summer, and the thin, white,.trembling hands were ever at work. But the brown hair turned gray rapidly, the easy-chair was relinquished for the bed, and before winter came the five children were left alone in the world. The wife had joined her husband. The ample estate that should have been theirs was gone. Strangers were in their home by the sea, and had divided out their lands; nor is it yet known whether they will be permitted to claim their inheritance.

This man, Colonel Edward B. Mallett, brave, beloved, lamented, was also a grandson of· the gay girl who had entertained Lord Cornwallis in her house near Cross Creek, and his fortunes were linked with those of the brother whose house and factory had been burned so lately. Thus did the destruction in one part of the State help on and intensify the ruin in another part.

Stories such as these are our inheritance from the great war; and yet, looking at the fate of those who have survived its dangers to be crushed by its issues, we may rather envy those who were laid sweetly to their rest while their hope for the country was not yet subjugated within them.

Let them rave !
Thou art quiet in thy grave.

CHAPTER VI.

BY the last of March General Sherman had entered Goldsboro, and effected his long meditated junction with General Schofield. He himself at once proceeded to Southern Virginia to hold a conference with General Grant, while the grand army lay quiet a few days to rest, recruit, and prepare for its further advance. Leaving them there, I venture to make a digression, suggested by the concluding lines of the preceding number of these sketches—a digression having for its object the consideration of the present policy of the Federal Government toward vanquished rebels, as compared with its policy in former cases of rebellion against its authority, even more inexcusable and unprovoked.

Chancellor Kent, adverting to the first rebellion against the government of this country, known in history as "Shays's Rebellion," pays the State of Massachusetts the following well-merited compliment on her conduct upon its suppression: "The clemency of Massachusetts in 1786, after an unprovoked and wanton rebellion, in not inflicting a single capital punishment, contributed, by the judicious manner in which its clemency was applied, to the more firm establishment of their government." (Com. on Am. Law. Vol. i. p. 283.) What were the circumstances of this first rebellion?

In 1786, the Legislature of that State laid taxes which were expected to produce near a million of dollars. The country had just emerged from the war of the Revolution in an exhausted and impoverished condition. Litigation abounded, and the people, galled by the pressure of their debts and of these taxes, manifested a spirit of revolt against their government. From loudly-expressed complaints they proceeded to meetings, and finally took up arms. They insisted that the courts should be closed; they clamored against the lawyers and their exorbitant fees, against salaried public officers; and they demanded the issue of paper money. The Governor of Massachusetts, John Bowdoin, convened the Legislature, and endeavored to allay the general and growing mutiny by concessions; but the excitement still increasing, the militia were ordered out, and Congress voted a supply of thirteen thousand men to aid the State Government. The leader of the insurrection was Daniel Shays, late a captain in the Continental army. At the head of one thousand men he prevented the session of the Supreme Court at Worcester, and his army soon increas-

ing to two thousand, they marched to Springfield, to
seize the national arsenal. Being promptly repulsed
by the commandant there, they fled, leaving several
killed and wounded. General Lincoln, at the head of
four thousand militia, pursued them to Amherst, and
thence to Pelham. On his approach they offered to
disperse on condition of a general pardon; but General Lincoln had no authority to treat. They then
retreated to Petersham. Lincoln pursued, and push-
ing on all night through intense cold and a driving
snow-storm, he accomplished an unprecedented march
of forty miles, and early next morning completely surprised the rebels in Petersham, taking one hundred
and fifty prisoners, and dispersing the rest so effectually that they never rallied again. Many took refuge
in New-Hampshire and the neighboring States, where
they were afterward arrested on requisition of Massachusetts. This ill-sustained and wanton rebellion was
easily quelled. Fourteen of the prisoners were con-
victed of treason, but not one was executed, and the
terms of pardon imposed were so moderate that eight
hundred took the benefit of them. Prudence dictated
this moderation and clemency, for it was known that
at least a third of the population sympathized with
the rebels. It was a significant fact that at the ensuing election, Governor Bowdoin, who had distinguished himself by his zeal and energy, was defeated, and
other public officers who had been especially active
against the rebels lost their seats, and were replaced
by more popular men. Daniel Shays lived to a good
old age, and died still in the enjoyment of his revolu-

tionary pension.* Such was the generous policy of a Northern government to Northern rebels in the first rebellion.

The second rebellion, commonly called the "Whisky Insurrection" of Western Pennsylvania, assumed more formidable proportions, and was instigated by even more sordid and inexcusable motives. In 1784, the distillers of that part of the State were resolved to deny the right of excise to the Federal Government. The excise law, though very unpopular, had been carried into execution in every part of the United States, and in most of the counties of Pennsylvania; but west of the Alleghany the people rose in arms against the Government officers, prevented them from exercising their functions, maltreated them, and compelled them to fly from the district, and finally called a meeting "to take into consideration the situation of the western country." They seized upon the mail, and opened the letters to discover what reports had been sent of their proceedings to Philadelphia, and by whom. They addressed a circular letter to the officers of the militia in the disaffected counties, calling on them to rendezvous at Braddock's Field on the first of August, with arms in good order, and four days' provisions, an "expedition," it was added, "in which they could have an opportunity of displaying their military talent, and of serving the country." This insurrection was headed by David Bradford, the prosecuting attorney

* For these particulars, I am indebted to Tucker's History of the United States, vol. i. chap. 4, and to Hildreth's History of the United States, first series, vol. iii. chap. 45.

for Washington county, and was secretly fomented by
agents of the French Republic, who desired nothing
better than to see the downfall of Washington's administration, and the reign of anarchy inaugurated on
this continent. A large body of men, estimated at
from five to ten thousand, met on the day appointed
at Braddock's Field. Bradford took upon himself the
military command. Albert Gallatin (lately a rejected
United States Senator, on the ground that he had not
been a resident of the State the length of time pre-
scribed for foreigners) was appointed Secretary.
"Cowards and traitors" were freely denounced, and
those who advocated moderate measures were over-
awed and silenced. The rioters then marched to Pitts-
burgh, which they would have burned but for the conciliatory conduct of the people of the town. They
burned the houses of several obnoxious men, compelled them to leave the country, and then dispersed.
It had been Bradford's design to get possession of
Fort Pitt, and seize the arms and ammunition there;
but not being supported in this by the militia officers,
he had abandoned it. All the remaining excise officers in the district were now forced to leave. Many
outrages were committed, houses burned, citizens insulted, and a reign of terror completely established.

The news of this formidable and wide-spread insurrection reaching Philadelphia, the President issued a
proclamation reciting the acts of treason, commanding
the insurgents to disperse, and warning others against
abetting them. This was the first of such proclamations ever issued in this country, and was no doubt

the model proposed to himself, and followed by President Lincoln in 1861. But Washington, at the same time, appointed three commissioners—a member of his cabinet, a Pennsylvania United States Senator, and a judge of the Supreme Court in that State—to repair to the scene of action, confer with the insurgents, and make every practicable attempt toward a peaceful adjustment. The policy of calling out the militia was discussed in the Cabinet. Hamilton and Knox were in favor of it. Randolph opposed it, and so did Governor Mifflin, who was consulted, on the ground that a resort to force might influence and augment the excitement and unite the whole State in rebellion. Washington finally determined to take the responsibility on himself and act with vigor, since if such open and daring resistance to the laws were not met and checked at once, it might find many imitators in other parts of the country, then so agitated and unsettled. The commissioners having failed to come to any satisfactory terms with the rebels, the opinion rapidly gained ground that the interposition of an armed force was indispensable. A body of fifteen thousand militia was called out from the States of Pennsylvania, New-Jersey, Maryland, and Virginia, and the whole force put under the command of Governor (and General) Henry Lee, of Virginia,* the father of *our*

* My readers will remember the reference in the second chapter to the capture by this officer of a portion of Tarleton's staff on Haw River, while engaged in satisfying the claims of a countryman for forage. No member of General Sherman's command is known to have suffered a surprise under similar circumstances. Certainly not in this region !

Washington's characteristic sagacity and humanity were shown in the selection of General Lee as commander of the forces.

General Robert E. Lee.   The news that this army was
on the march materially increased the numbers and
influence of the moderate party in Western Pennsylvania.   The Standing Committee of the insurgents
met and recommended submission, which was ably
and zealously advocated by Albert Gallatin and
Breckenridge.   Nothing decisive was agreed upon,
and pending another convention, many of the ring-
leaders fled from the State; David Bradford, who had
been foremost among them, being the first to seek
safety in flight to New-Orleans.

A resolution of submission wàs passed at the second
convention, and a committtee of two, one of whom,
Findley, was a member of Congress, appointed to con-
vey it to the President at Carlisle.   The President received this committee courteously, but the march of
the troops was not arrested.   A third convention being held, and resolutions to pay all excise duties and
recommending the surrender of all delinquents having
passed, General Lee issued a proclamation granting an
amnesty to all who had submitted, and calling on the
people to take the oath of allegiance to the United
States.   Orders were issued and executed to seize
those offenders who had not submitted, and send them
to Philadelphia.   Of those who were tried before the
Circuit Court, only two were found guilty of capital
offenses, one of arson and the other of robbing the
mail; and both were ultimately pardoned by the
President.   In less than four months from the burning
of the first house, the insurrection was completely defeated, and entire order restored.   A force of twenty-

five hundred militia was retained in the disaffected district during the ensuing winter, under command of General Morgan. Provision was made to indemnify those whose property had been destroyed, and an appropriation of more than a million of dollars was made by Congress to defray the expenses incurred. Albert Gallatin, who was then a hardly naturalized foreigner, notwithstanding the part he had taken in the earlier stages of the rebellion, by his subsequent moderate counsels had regained the confidence of the Government, and being the choice of the people of that district, was elected to the next Congress, taking his seat without any opposition or word of rebuke. His subsequent brilliant career is now part of our national history. Findley, who was a member of Congress at the time of the outbreak, and was at one time prominent among the sympathizers, though he acted at no time with decision, did not forfeit his seat by his participation in the revolt. He appeared in his place in Congress the ensuing November. He afterward wrote an elaborate history of the insurrection and a vindication of himself and his friends. According to him the troops sent to quell the rebellion would have left more emphatic tokens of their desire for vengeance on the rebels, "if it had not been for the moderation of Washington and his resistless weight of character in the execution of his purposes."*

The prompt, energetic, and efficient measures of the Administration in arresting the progress of this re-

* Tucker's History, vol. i. chap. 7. Hildreth's History, second series, vol. i. chap. 7.

volt, and its magnanimity and moderation toward the offenders afterward, contributed very materially to strengthen the Government at a critical period of its existence, to give it dignity and influence, and to rally round it the best affections of the people. And its patience and forbearance had been somewhat tried by the State of Pennsylvania in those days. There had been many symptoms of instability in the " Keystone" of the newly-erected arch of civil liberty. There were two examples of mutiny among the Pennsylvania troops during the Revolution, and two popular insurrections in regard to the excise laws, and this one had opened with the exhibition of a temper ferocious and reckless. The estimate by the Administration of the danger of the rebellion in 1794 may be inferred from the fact that the number of troops called for to suppress it was greater, in proportion to the then population of the United States, than the call made by President Lincoln in 1861 to the present population. In 1790, the white population of the United States was 3,172,464. The troops called out in '94 were 15,000. In 1860, the white population was 26,690,206. Troops ordered out, 75,000. The proportion in 1794 was greater, according to these figures, in the ratio of 389 to 354, without allowing for increase from 1790 to '94. And the magnitude of the danger did indeed fully justify all the apprehensions and precautions of the guardians of the state. The young republic was but newly formed, the Government scarcely settled. Many prominent and able men in different parts of the country were turning admiring eyes toward France in her wild career, others toward some vision of a monarchical form. Emissaries from the distracted states of the Old World were prompt and zealous to foment discords and disturbances, and precedents were wanting every day to meet new issues that arose continually. The situation needed all the wisdom, prudence, and magnanimity of the illustrious man called by Providence to guide the first steps of a great nation.

Does any one hesitate to believe that if we had had a Washington for President in 1860 and 1861, the late war would never have taken place ; that secession would never have been accomplished ? How vigorous and yet how conciliatory would have been the measures. The seventy-five thousand would no doubt have been called for, but commissioners of peace to the "wayward sisters" would have preceded them. In our day it was the insurgents who sent commissioners. The best men of the South were a month in Washington City, vainly endeavoring for a hearing, vainly hoping for some offer of conciliation or adjustment, and deluded by promises from the highest officials that were never meant to be fulfilled.

Does any one doubt what would have been Washington's conduct of the grand army through its unparalleled and immortal march of triumph ? Even had he not been guided by Christian principles of honor and humanity, he would at least have emulated the example and shared the glory of the noble heathen of whom it was said : " *Postremo signa, et tabulas, ceteraque ornamenta Græcorum oppidorum, quæ ceteri tollenda esse arbitrantur, ea sibi ille ne visenda quidem existimavit. Itaque omnes quidem nunc in his locis Cn. Pompeium sicut aliquem non ex hac urbe missum, sed de cœlo delapsum, intuentur."**

And finally, can any one doubt what his policy would now be toward the people so lately in arms against their Government? Alas! to him alone, first in war and first in peace, can the whole of the splendid eulogy of the Roman orator to the great captain of *his* day be fittingly applied: "*Humanitati jam tantâ est, ut difficile dictu sit, utrum hostes magis virtutem ejus pugnantis timuerint, an mansuetudinem victi delixerint.*"†

Just twenty years from the time of the second rebellion, the third, and by far the most evil-disposed, malignant, and far-reaching expression of hostility to the General Government was organized. The Hartford Convention indeed never proceeded so far as to make an appeal to arms, but the spirit that suggested it, and the temper displayed by its leaders, give it undoubtedly the best claim to have inaugurated the hateful doctrine of secession.

The war of 1812 with England was, in general, excessively unpopular in the New-England States. Their commerce was burned; their fisheries were broken up, and their merchants and ship-owners, who

---

* "Lastly, the statues and pictures and other ornaments of Grecian cities, which other commanders suppose might be carried off, he indeed thought that they ought not even to have been looked at by him. Therefore now all the inhabitants in those places look upon Cn. Pompey as one not sent from this city, but descended from heaven."

† "Now, by the exercise of such great humanity it has become hard to say whether his enemies feared his valor more when they were fighting, or loved his humanity more when they were conquered."

constituted the wealthiest and most influential class among them, were heavy losers. The Administration had always been unpopular with them, and now its policy of embargo, non-importation, non-intercourse, and finally of war, were sufficient to rouse them into active opposition. This was manifested in various ways; in the annual addresses of their governors; in reports of legislative committees; in laws to embarrass the action of the Federal Executive, as, for instance, forbidding it the use of any of their jails for the confinement of prisoners of war, and ordering all their jailers to liberate all British prisoners committed to their keeping; in refusing to contribute their quota of men for the support of the war, and even to allow them to march beyond the limits of their own State. The spirit of disaffection was diligently cherished by the leaders, and went on increasing in bitterness and extent till a convention was proposed and agreed upon. On the 15th of December, 1814, there assembled in the city of Hartford twelve delegates from Massachusetts, seven from Connecticut, four from Rhode Island, three county delegates from New-Hampshire, and one from Vermont. They sat with closed doors till the 5th of January, 1815, when they adjourned, having issued a report setting forth their grievances and aims. The following extract from a report of the proceedings of the Legislature will exhibit the spirit that prevailed through the State:

" We believe that this war, so fertile in calamities, and so threatening in its consequences, has been waged with the worst possible views, and carried on in the

worst possible manner, forming a union of wickedness
and weakness which defies, for a parallel, the annals
of the world. We believe also that its worst effects
are yet to come; that loan upon loan, tax upon tax,
and exaction upon exaction, must be imposed, until the
comforts of the present and the hopes of the rising
generation are destroyed. *An impoverished people will
be an enslaved people.*" Of the right of the State to
prevent the exercise of unconstitutional power by the
General Government, they had no doubt. " A power
to regulate commerce is abused when employed to destroy it, and a voluntary abuse of power sanctions the
right of resistance as much as a direct and palpable
usurpation. The sovereignty reserved to the States
was reserved to protect the citizens from acts of violence by the United States, as well as for purposes of
domestic regulation. We spurn the idea that the
free, sovereign, and independent State of Massachusetts is reduced to a mere municipal corporation, without power to protect its people, or to defend them
from oppression, from whatever quarter it comes.
Whenever the national compact is violated, and the
citizens of this State oppressed by cruel and unauthorized enactments, this Legislature is bound to interpose
its power, and to wrest from the oppressor its victim.
This is the spirit of our Union."

The manifesto of the Convention did not, could not,
use stronger language. After proposing seven amendments to the Constitution, and giving reasons for their
adoption, they disclaimed all hostility to that Constitution, and professed only to aim to unite all the

friends of the country of all parties, and obtain their aid in effecting a change of Federal rulers. Should this be hopeless, they hinted at the "necessity of more mighty efforts," which were plainly set forth in their resolutions, and everywhere understood to refer to a secession of the five New-England States, their consolidation into an independent government of their own, or alliance with England.*

The time chosen for such a display of enmity to the Union was most opportune for the purposes of the traitors. A war with a foreign foe, and that foe the most powerful nation on earth, was in progress; the Administration was greatly embarrassed ; the country was rent with fierce party factions. What would be the issue no human wisdom could foresee ; but that the ruin of the country was not then effected, can not be attributed to the patriotism of the New-England States. Three commissioners, appointed by the Governor of Massachusetts, to whom Connecticut added two others, proceeded to Washington to lay their resolutions and applications before the Government. But, most happily, news of the treaty of Ghent and consequent peace arriving at the same time with these envoys, their mission became the theme of unsparing taunt and ridicule in the papers, and they returned home without disburdening themselves of their object. Thus the third rebellion was snuffed out by events ; but its sparks were blown far and wide by viewless winds, and effected a lodgment where, though smoth-

* Tucker's History, vol. iii. chap. 18.   Hildreth, vol. iii. chap. 29.

ered for a generation or two, they yet burned in secret, and at length burst out in the great conflagration of 1860, which lit the whole horizon and dyed the very heavens with its crimson. The principles of the Hartford Convention were the seeds of nullification and secession.

The eminent historian from Massachusetts records in glowing pages the stifling of the earliest throbs of civil and religious liberty on this continent in 1676. The earliest martyr in the Bacon Rebellion against monarchical tyranny was William Drummond, the first Governor of North-Carolina. His name is written on the beautiful sheet of water that lies within the tangled brakes of the great swamp on the bordes rof the land he loved and served so well. In that rebellion the women (as at this day) shared the popular enthusiasm. "The child that is unborn," said Sarah Drummond, "shall rejoice for the good that will come by the rising of the country." She would not suffer a throb of fear in her bosom, and in the greatest perils to which her husband was exposed, she confidently exclaimed, "We shall do well enough," and continually encouraged the people and inspired the soldiers with her own enthusiasm. When Edmund Cheesman was arraigned for trial, his wife declared that but for her he never would have joined the rebellion, and on her knees begged that she might bear the punishment. Yet these devoted people saw the cause for which they had risked and lost every thing in the dust, overthrown, and trampled upon with vindictive fury by the triumphant royalists. In the judicial trials

that followed, a rigor and merciless severity were exhibited, worthy of the gloomy judge whose "bloody
assize," ten years later, on the western circuit of England, has left an indelible blot on her history. Twenty-
two were hanged; three others died of cruelty in
prison; three more fled before trial; two escaped after
conviction. Nor is it certain when Sir William Berkeley's thirst for blood would have been appeased if the
newly convened assembly had not voted an address
that the Governor "should spill no more blood." On
Berkeley's return to England he was received with
coldness, and his cruelty openly disavowed by the government. "That old fool," said the kind-hearted
Charles II., "has taken more lives in that naked country than I for the murder of my father." *

"More blood was shed," adds the historian, "than,
on the action of our present political system, would be
shed for political offenses in a thousand years." Alas!
for the sunny South, the scorched and consumed South,
alas for her! that the prediction of the great American historian is not history!

Considering this rebellion in the perspective afforded by nearly two hundred years, it is easy for us to
understand how the severity with which it was punished by the fanatic old royal Governor only drove
the entering-wedge of separation between the mother
country and her colonies in America deeper. The
principles of Bacon and his party had obtained a great
hold on the popular mind; and though for years all

* Bancroft's History, vol. ii. chap. 14.

tendency to a popular government appeared to be crushed out and forever silenced, yet they were there, in the hearts of men, silently growing, nurtured by a deep sense of injustice and wrong, and biding their time. Just a century from the suppression of the " Baconists," the Declaration of Independence was adopted ; Sarah Drummond's words were verified, and Bacon and Drummond and Cheesman and Hansford were amply avenged.

It is to such pages of history as these that I would turn the attention of our Northern friends now. Here they may see how the Father of his country dealt with his wayward children. How a prompt and dignified and successful assertion of the rights of the Federal Government were followed by leniency and generous and prudent forbearance such as a great government can afford to show, and by which it best exhibits its strength and its claims to the love and veneration of its people. Here they may see how a brutal gratification of vengeance, a lust of blood, like the tiger's spring, overleaps its mark. The hardest lesson to be learned is moderation in the hour of triumph ; the greatest victory to be achieved is the victory over self.

Where now are the Bowdoins, the Hancocks, the Dexters, the Ames, the Websters of Massachusetts ? Has she no statesman now capable of rising to the magnanimity which characterized her early history ? Has thrice revolting and thrice pardoned Pennsylvania no representative man who can rise to the height of the great argument, and vindicate the cause of a country pillaged and plundered and peeled to an extent of which the history of civilized humanity affords us no parallel? Is there no one now to stand up and advocate for Southerners the same measure of forbearance and generosity that was shown by a Southern President to Northern rebels?

"O thou that spoilest and wast not spoiled, that dealt treacherously, and they dealt not treacherously with thee!" haste to the work of reconciliation and to build up the waste places! Even now on our thresholds are heard the sounds of the departing feet of those who in despair for their country, hopeless of peace or of justice, are leaving our broad, free, noble land for the semi-civilized haciendas of Mexico or of far-off tropical Brazil. Even now are their journals scattered freely among us—invitations, beckonings, sneers at the North, flattery of the South, fair promises, golden lures, every inducement held out to a high-hearted and fainting people to cast their lot in with them. Haste to arrest them by some display of returning fraternity and consideration, ere for them we raise the saddest lament yet born of the war: "Weep ye not for the dead, neither bemoan him; but weep sore for him that goeth away, for he shall return no more, nor see his native country!"

CHAPTER VII.

THE town of Goldsboro was occupied by General
Schofield's army on the twenty-first of March. No
resistance was offered by the Confederates, who had
withdrawn in the direction of Smithfield, with the exception of one regiment of cavalry, which had a slight
skirmish with Schofield's advance near the town.
General Schofield's conduct toward the citizens of the
town was conciliatory. No plundering was allowed
by him; efficient guards were stationed, and beyond
the loss of fences and outhouses torn down for firing,
etc., depredations on poultry-yards, etc., and a few
smoke-houses, there was but little damage done. But
in the surrounding country the outrages were innumer-
able, and in many places the desolation complete. On
the twenty-third of March General Sherman's grand
army made its appearance, heralded by the columns
of smoke which rose from burning farm-houses on the
south side of the Neuse. For thirty-six hours they
poured in, in one continuous stream. Every available

spot in the town, and for miles around it, was covered
with the two armies, estimated at one hundred and
twenty-five thousand men. General Sherman's reputation had preceded him, and the horror and dismay
with which his approach was anticipated in the country were fully warranted. The town itself was in a
measure defended, so to speak, by General Schofield's
preöccupation; but in the vicinity and for twenty miles
round, the country was most thoroughly plundered
and stripped of food, forage, and private property of
every description. One of the first of General Sherman's own acts, after his arrival, was of peculiar hardship. One of the oldest and most venerable citizens
of the place, with a family of sixteen or eighteen children and grandchildren, most of them females, was ordered, on a notice of a few hours, to vacate his house,
for the convenience of the General himself, which of
course was done. The gentleman was nearly eighty
years of age, and in very feeble health. The out-
houses, fences, grounds, etc., were destroyed, and the
property greatly damaged during its occupation by
the General. Not a farm-house in the country but
was visited and wantonly robbed. Many were burned, and very many, together with out-houses, were
pulled down and hauled into camps for use. Generally not a live animal, not a morsel of food of any
description was left, and in many instances not a bed
or sheet or change of clothing for man, woman, or
child. It was most heart-rending to see daily crowds
of country people, from three-score and ten years of
age, down to the unconscious infant carried in its

mother's arms, coming into the town to beg food and shelter, to ask alms from those who had despoiled them. Many of these families lived for days on parched corn, on peas boiled in water without salt, on scraps picked up about the camps. The number of carriages, buggies, and wagons brought in is almost incredible. They kept for their own use what they wished, and burned or broke up the rest. General Logan and staff took possession of seven rooms in the house of John C. Slocumb, Esq., the gentleman of whose statements I avail myself. Every assurance of protection was given to the family by the quartermaster; but many indignities were offered to the inmates, while the house was as effectually stripped as any other of silver plate, watches, wearing apparel, and money. Trunks and bureaus were broken open and the contents abstracted. Not a plank or rail or post or paling was left anywhere upon the grounds, while fruit-trees, vines, and shrubbery were wantonly destroyed. These officers remained nearly three weeks, occupying the family beds, and when they left the bed-clothes also departed.

It is very evident that General Sherman entered North-Carolina with the confident expectation of receiving a welcome from its Union-loving citizens. In Major Nichols's story of the Great March, he remarks, on crossing the line which divides South from North-Carolina : "The conduct of the soldiers is perceptibly changed. I have seen no evidence of plundering, the men keep their ranks closely; and more remarkable yet, not a single column of the fire or smoke which a few days ago marked the positions of the heads of columns, can be seen upon the horizon. Our men seem to understand that they are entering a State which has suffered for its Union sentiment, and whose inhabitants would gladly embrace the old flag again if they can have the opportunity, which we mean to give them," (page 222.) But the town-meeting and war resolutions of the people of Fayetteville, the fight in her streets, and Governor Vance's proclamation, soon undeceived them, and their amiable dispositions were speedily corrected and abandoned.

On first entering our State, Major Nichols, looking sharply about him, and fortunately disposed to do justice, under the impression that he was among friends, declares: "It is not in our imagination alone that we can at once see a difference between South and North-Carolina. The soil is not superior to that near Cheraw, but the farmers are a vastly different class of men. I had always supposed that South-Carolina was agriculturally superior to its sister State. The loud pretensions of the chivalry had led me to believe that the scorn of these gentlemen was induced by the inferiority of the people of the old North State, and that they were little better than ' dirt-eaters;' but the strong Union sentiment which has always found utterance here should have taught me better. The real difference between the two regions lies in the fact that here the plantation owners work with their own hands, and do not think they degrade themselves thereby. For the first time since we bade farewell to salt water, I have to-day seen an attempt to manure land. The army has passed through thirteen miles or more of splendidly-managed plantations ; the corn and cotton-fields are nicely plowed and furrowed ; the fences are in capital order ; the barns are well built ; the dwelling-houses are cleanly, and there is that air of thrift which shows that the owner takes a personal interest in the management of affairs," (page 222.)

It happens curiously enough that North-Carolina, ninety-two years ago, made much the same impression on a stranger then traveling peacefully through her eastern border ; and his record is worth comparing with the foregoing, as showing that her State individuality was as strongly and clearly defined then as now, and that the situation of our people in 1773 closely resembled in some particulars that of their descendants in 1865.

" The soils and climates of the Carolinas differ, but not so much as their inhabitants. The number of negroes and slaves is much less in North than in South-Carolina. Their staple commodity is not so valuable, not being in so great demand as the rice, indigo, etc., of the South. Hence labor becomes more necessary, and he who has an interest of his own to serve is a laborer in the field. Husbandmen and agriculture increase in number and improvement. Industry is up in the woods at tar, pitch, and turpentine; in the fields plowing, planting, clearing, or fencing the land. Herds and flocks become more numerous. You see husbandmen, yeomen, and white laborers scattered through the country instead of herds of negroes and slaves. Healthful countenances and numerous fami-

lies become more common as you advance. Property
is much more equally diffused through one province
than in the other, and this may account for some if
not all the differences of character in the inhabitants.
The people of the Carolinas certainly vary much as
to their general sentiments, opinions, and judgments;
and there is very little intercourse between them.
The present State of North-Carolina is really curi-
ous; there are but five provincial laws in force through
the colony, and no courts at all in being. No one can
recover a debt, except before a single magistrate, where
the sums are within his jurisdiction, and offenders
escape with impunity. The people are in great con-
sternation about the matter; what will be the conse-
quence is problematical." (*Memoir of Josiah Quincy,*
Jr., page 123.) The situation of North-Carolina during the last eight months of 1865 furnishes an exact
parallel to the above concluding paragraph, and the
whole may be taken as a.fair illustration of the oft-
repeated sentiment that history but repeats itself.

Major Nichols's impression of the old North State
would scarcely have been so favorably expressed had
he known what reception her people were to give the
grand army. One week later, he writes: " Thus far
we have been painfully disappointed in looking for
the Union sentiment in North-Carolina, about which
so much has been said. Our experience is decidedly
in favor of its sister State. The city of Fayetteville
was offensively rebellious;" and further on, " The
rebels have shown more pluck at Averasboro and at
Bentonsville than we have encountered since leaving
Atlanta."

While the Federal armies lay at Goldsboro, trains were running day and night from Beaufort and from Wilmington, conveying stores for the supply and complete refit of Sherman's army. The Confederate army, lying between Goldsboro and Raleigh, having no supplies or reënforcements to receive, waited grimly and despairingly the order to fall back upon Raleigh, which came as soon as General Sherman, having effected his interview with General Grant, had returned to Goldsboro, with his future plan of action matured, and once more, on the tenth of April, set the grand army in motion. The scenes in Raleigh during the first week of April were significant enough. The removal of government stores, and of the effects of the banks; the systematic concealment of private property of every description; the hurried movements of troops to and fro; the doubt, dismay, and gloom painted on every man's face, told but too well the story of anticipated defeat and humiliation. If there were any who secretly exulted in the advance of the Federal army, they were not known. The nearest approach to any such feeling in any respectable man's breast was probably the not unnatural sense of satisfaction with which men who had long seen their opinions derided and execrated now felt that their hour of vindication was arriving, the hour which every thoughtful man in the State had long since foreseen. The united North was too strong for the South, and the weaker cause—whether right or wrong—was doomed. I repeat, not a thoughtful or clear-headed man in North-Carolina but had foreseen this result as most probable, while at the same time not a thoughtful man or respectable citizen within our borders but had considered it his duty as well as his interest to stand by his State and do all in his power to assist her in the awful struggle. Till the Northern people, as a body, can understand how it was that such conflicting emotions held sway among us, and can see how an honorable people could resist and deplore secession, and yet fight to the last gasp in support of the Confederacy, and in obedience to the laws of the State, it is idle to hope for a fair judgment from them. This, however, contradictory as it may seem to superficial observers, was the position of North-Carolina all through the war, from its wild inception to its sullen close, and as such was defended and illustrated by her best and ablest statesmen. Foremost and most earnest in her efforts to maintain peace and preserve the Union—for she was the only State which sent delegates to both the Northern and Southern peace conventions—she was yet foremost also in the fight and freest in her expenditure of blood and treasure to sustain the common cause, which she had so reluctantly embraced ; and now the time was fast approaching when she was again to vindicate her claims to supreme good sense and discretion, by being among the first to admit the hopelessness and sin of further effort, and the first to offer and accept the olive-branch.

Frequently during the winter of 1864–65, had the eyes of our people been turned toward our Senator in the Confederate Congress, anxious for some public expression of opinion as to the situation from him, waiting to see what course he would indicate as most proper and honorable. For of those who stood foremost as representative North-Carolinians, of those who possessed the largest share of personal popularity and influence in the State, it is not too much to say that Ex-Governor GRAHAM was by far the most conspicuous and preëminent—the man of whom it may be said more truly than of any other, that as he spoke so North-Carolina felt, and as he acted, so North-Carolina willed. And now, in the approaching crisis, there was no man by whose single deliberate judgment the whole State would have so unanimously agreed to be guided.

It may be well to pause here and glance at Governor Graham's antecedents and associations, the better to understand his claims to such prominence and such influence.

In a country such as ours, where hereditary distinctions do not exist, it is peculiarly pleasant to observe such a transmission of principles, and virtues, and talents, as is exhibited in the Graham family. The father of Governor Graham was General Joseph Graham, of Revolutionary fame, than whom there did not exist a more active and able partisan leader in North-Carolina. In the affair at Charlotte in 1780, referred to in a preceding number, when one hundred and fifty militia, under Colonel Davie, gave the whole British army under Cornwallis such a warm reception, most efficient aid was rendered by Major Joseph Graham, who commanded a small company of volunteers on that occasion. He was covered with wounds, and his recovery was considered by his friends as little short of miraculous. But he was afterward distinguished in many heroic exploits, and commanded in no less than fifteen different engagements.

His youngest son, William Alexander, was born in 1804, in Lincoln county, graduated at the State University in 1824, chose the profession of the law, and entered upon public life as member of the General Assembly in 1833, three years before the death of his venerable father. The talents, patriotism, and energy which had distinguished the Revolutionary patriot, were transmitted in full measure to his son, and North-Carolina evinced her appreciation of his abilities by retaining him in public office whenever he would consent to serve, from the time of his first entrance. And Governor Graham has never failed, has never been unequal to the occasion, or to the expectations formed of him, however high. His very appearance gives assurance of the energy, calm temper, high ability, and nerve which have always characterized him. As a lawyer and advocate, his reputation is eminent and his success brilliant ; but it is as a statesman that his career is particularly to be noted now. He was United States Senator in 1840, elected Governor of the State in 1844, and reëlected in 1846. His immediate predecessor in this office was the Hon J. M. Morehead, previously referred to as a member of the Peace Convention at Washington ; and his successor was the Hon. Charles Manly—all Whigs—and Governor Manly, the last of that school of politics elected to that office, previous to the civil war. Governor Graham was appointed Secretary of the Navy in 1850, by President Fillmore, which he resigned in 1852 on receiving the nomination for Vice-President on the ticket with General Scott. He was repeatedly member of the General Assembly, and in all positions has merited and enjoyed the fullest and most unhesitating confidence of the people he represented, worthy of them and worthy of his parentage.

His connection in politics having been ever with the Whig party, he was thereby removed in the furthest possible degree from any countenance to the doctrines of Nullification and Secession. Hence he had concurred with Webster's great speech in reply to Hayne in 1830, with the proclamation of Jackson in 1832, with Clay in 1850, and with the entire policy of President Fillmore's eminently national administration. In February, 1860, he visited Washington City to consult with such friends as Crittenden of Kentucky, Rives of Virginia, and Granger of New-York, on the dangers then environing and threatening the country, the result of which was a convention nominating Bell and Everett for the Presidential ticket, with the motto, "The Union, the Constitution, and the enforcement of the laws." He canvassed the State on his return home, for these candidates and principles, warning the people, however, that there was a likelihood of Mr. Lincoln's election; and that in such a case it was evidently the purpose of the Secessionists who supported Breckinridge, to break up the Government and involve the country in civil war. Party, however, was at that time stronger than patriotism, and Breckinridge carried the State. On Mr.

Lincoln's election, Governor Graham made public addresses, exhorting the people to submit and yield due obedience to his office. When the Legislature that winter ordered an election to take the sense of the people on the call of a convention, and at the same time to elect delegates, Governor Graham opposed the call, and it was signally defeated in the State. He was proposed as a Commissioner to the Peace Convention at Washington, but was rejected by the secessionist majority because of his decided and openly expressed Union sentiments.

After the attack on Fort Sumter, and the secession of Virginia and of Tennessee, leaving North-Carolina perfectly isolated among the seceded States, and with civil war already begun, Governor Graham decided to adopt the cause of the Southern States, but with pain and reluctance, not upon any pretense of right, but as a measure of revolution, and of national interest and safety. He was a member of the convention which in May, 1861, carried the State out of the Union, and from the date of the secession ordinance he endeavored in good faith and honor to sustain the cause of the Confederate States, but without any surrender on the part of the people of the rights and liberties of freemen. In the Convention of 1862, he delivered an elaborate speech in opposition to test oaths, sedition laws, the suspension of the privilege of *habeas corpus*, and all abridgments of the constitutional rights of the citizen, either by State conventions, or by Legislatures, or by Congress, which may be safely pronounced the clearest and ablest vindication of the cardinal principles of civil liberty presented in the annals of the Confederacy.

The expression of such views, such an evident determination that the country should be free, not only in the end, but in the means, coupled with great moderation of opinion as to the final result of the struggle, and a total absence of all fire-eating proclivities, drew down upon him the free criticism of the secession press and party, many of whom did not hesitate to brand him as a traitor to the cause, notwithstanding the assurances he gave of five sons in the army, some one of whom was in every important battle on the Atlantic slope, except Bull Run and Chancellorsville ; two being present when the flag of Lee went down on his last battle-field at Appomattox, while a third then lay languishing with a severe and recent wound at Petersburg. Governor Graham's sons derived no advantage from their father's distinguished position in North-Carolina. They received no favors or patronage from the Government, but were engaged in arduous and perilous service all through, in such subordinate offices as were conferred by the election of their comrades, or in the ordinary course of promotion.

No families in the State gave more freely of their best blood and treasure in the support of the war than the Graham family and its connections. Governor Graham's younger sister, Mrs. Morrison, wife of the Rev. Dr. Morrison, of Lincoln county, the first President of Davidson College, had three sons in the service, and four sons-in-law, namely, Major Avery, General Barringer, General D. H. Hill, and *O præclarum et venerabile nomen*, STONEWALL JACKSON! Perhaps no two families entered upon the rebellion more re-luctantly, nor in their whole course were more entirely in unison with the views and feelings of the great body of our citizens.

Major Avery, the youngest of Dr. Morrison's sons-in-law, was one of five brothers, sons of Colonel Isaac T. Avery, of Burke; grandsons of Colonel Waightstill Avery, who commanded a regiment during the revo-lutionary war, and was a member of the Mecklenburg Convention, and a colleague there of Major Robert Davidson, Mrs. Morrison's maternal grandfather. Three of these five brothers fell in battle. The youngest, Colonel Isaac T. Avery, named for his father, fell at Gettysburgh. He survived his wounds a few minutes, long enough to beckon to his lieuten-ant-colonel for a pencil and a scrap of paper, on which with his dying fingers he assured his father that he died doing his whole duty. His father, approaching his eightieth year, received the note, stained with his son's life-blood, and died a few weeks afterward. The oldest of the brothers, Waightstill, named for his grandfather, and the pride of the family, was a son-in-law of ·Governor Morehead, and his colleague in the first Confederate Congress. He fell· in Kirk's raid near Morganton. Governor Morehead,* who was, with the exception of the distinguished President of the University, Governor Swain, the oldest of the surviv-ing ex-governors of the State, had two sons and two

* This distinguished gentleman has departed this life since these sketches were first published in THE WATCHMAN.—EDITOR.

sons-in-law in the army; the two latter were killed.
Govornor Graham's immediate successor as governor
—Charles Manly, of Raleigh—had three sons in the
army, all of whom saw hard service; and three sons-
in-law, two of whom were killed. There were not
wanting those in the dark hours of the contest who
spoke of it as "the rich man's war, and the poor man's
fight." These examples show that it was the war of
all. The rich and the poor met together, and mingled
their blood in a common current, and lie together
among the unrecorded dead. The history of many
families may be traced whose sacrifices were similar
to the above instances. And it is now the imperative
duty of those fitted for the work, to gather up these
records for posterity, and for the future historian and
annalist of the country. Many striking coïncidences
and connections in family history, many most affecting instances of unselfish devotion and of irreparable
loss, are yet to be preserved by hands eager

> "To light the flame of a soldier's fame
> On the turf of a soldier's grave."

CHAPTER VIII.

WHATEVER distrust of Governor Graham was manifested by those who had invoked the war, he was
fully sustained by the people ; for the adoption of the
ordinance of secession by no means implied the acces-
sion of secessionists to power in the State. That
step having been taken, the Confederate Constitution
ratified, and the honor and future destiny of our people being staked on the revolution, Governor Graham
stood prepared to devote all the energies of the State
to give it success ; and the mass of the people, not being willing to forgive the authors of the movement,
demanded the services of the Union men who had embraced it as a necessity. Governor Graham was sent
from the Legislature by a majority of three fourths to
the Confederate Senate, in December, 1863, on the resignation of the Hon. George Davis, who had accepted
the appointment of Attorney-General in the Cabinet
of President Davis. Before the commencement of his

term, (May, 1864,) by means of conscription and impressment laws, and the suspension of *habeas corpus*, the whole population and resources of the country had been placed at the command of the President for the prosecution of the war. The implicit and entire surrender by the whole Southern people of their dearest civil rights and liberties, of their lives and property into the hands of the Government, for the support of a war, which, it may be safely asserted, the large majority were opposed to, will form a field of curious and interesting speculation to the future historian and philosopher. There can not be a higher compliment paid to the character of our people, and the principles in which they had been nurtured, than the fact that no intestine disorders or disasters followed, upon such extraordinary demands of power on the one part, and such extraordinary resignation of rights on the other. Whatever the Confederate Government asked for its own security, the people gave, and gave freely to the last.

The defeats at Gettysburgh and Vicksburgh had turned the tide of success in favor of the North, and although this was partially relieved by the minor victories of Plymouth and elsewhere, the hopes of ultimate success were becoming much darkened. Governor Graham had never doubted that the North had the physical ability to conquer, if her people could be kept up to a persevering effort, nor that our only chances depended on their becoming wearied of the contest. As our fortunes lowered, all men of prevision and sagacity turned their thoughts toward the possibility of over-

tures for peace as becoming daily of greater importance and more imminent necessity.   But how could
this be done ?   With a powerful enemy pressing us,
with war established by law, with entire uncertainty
as to the terms to be expected in case of submission,
with the necessity imposed of making no public de-
monstration which should dampen the ardor of our
troops, or depress still further the spirits of our people, and excite the hopes of the enemy ; with such
obstacles in the way, peace could not be approached
by a public man without involving the risk of in-
augurating greater evils than those he sought to avert.
Besides all this, by the adoption of the Constitution
of the Confederate States, (which, by the way, Governor Graham had vainly endeavored to prevent in
convention, without a second,) all legal power to ter-
minate the war had been surrendered to the President.
Any other method would have been revolutionary, and
have provoked civil strife among us, and, doubtless,
sharp retribution.

The only plan, therefore, which could afford reasonable hope of success was to operate upon and through
the President.   This was attempted at the first session
of Congress of which Governor Graham was a member, by secret resolutions introduced by Mr. Orr, the
present Governor of South-Carolina, which, however,
failed to get a majority vote of the Senate.   Governor
Graham, who was deeply impressed with a sense of
the absolute necessity of some movement toward
peace, and who was not among the confidential friends
of the President, attempted next to operate on him

through those who were in some measure influential with him.   By this means he had an agency in setting on foot the mission to Fortress Monroe, the result of which is well known.   In the absence of Mr. Hunter on that mission, Governor Graham was president *pro tem.* of the Senate.   Disappointed and mortified by that failure, he then approached President Davis directly, and the results were stated in his private correspondence with a confidential friend in North-Carolina.   There can be no better exponent of Governor Graham's position and views at this momentous crisis in our history, than is found in these letters, and I esteem myself peculiarly fortunate in being able to present to my readers such extracts from them as will assist my purpose.   They are the letters of a consummate statesman, and of a patriot, and need no heralding :

RICHMOND, January 28, 1865.

MY DEAR SIR : The intervention of F. P. Blair, who has passed two or three times back and forth from Washington to this city recently, has resulted in the appointment to-day by the President of an informal commission, consisting of Messrs. A. H. Stephens, R. M. T. Hunter, and J. A. Campbell, to proceed to Washington and confer with a like band there, on the subject-matters of difference between the Northern and Southern States, with a view to terms of peace. The action of the Senate was not invoked, it is presumed because the appointment of formal ministers might be considered inadmissible until the question of recognition should be settled in our favor.   I trust that a termination of hostilities will be the result. From several conversations with Mr. Hunter, in concert with whom I have been endeavoring to reach this form of intercourse since the commencement of the session of Congress, I am satisfied that the first effort will be to establish an armistice of as long duration as may be allowed, and then to agree upon terms of settlement. Upon the latter I anticipate great conflict of views. The Northern mind is wedded to the idea of reconstruction, and notwithstanding the violence of the extravagant Republicans, I am convinced would guarantee slavery as it now exists, and probably make other concessions, including of course, amnesty, restoration of confiscated property, except slaves, and perhaps some compensation for a part of these. On the other hand, while the people of the South are wearied of the war, and are ready to make the greatest sacrifice to end it, there are embarrassments attending the abdication of a great government such as now wields the power of the South, especially by the agents appointed to maintain it, that are difficult to overcome. The commission is a discreet one, and upon the whole is as well constituted as I expected, and I trust that good will come of it. I have not seen any of the gentlemen since hearing to-day of their appointment, and I learn they are to set off to-morrow. I am therefore ignorant of the instructions they may carry, if any have been given. The Vice-President was not on terms with the head of the Government until a reconciliation yesterday. Although the North would seem to be bent on war unless and until the Union be restored, they yet regard us as a formidable foe, and I suspect the ruling authorities estimate our power as highly as it deserves. The Secretary of State here, I understand, says they have been frightened into negotiations by the articles in the Richmond *Enquirer*, threatening a colonial connection with England and France ; while others, I hear from Mr. Rives, assert that the North is much troubled by the proposition to make soldiers of slaves. I have no faith in either of these fancies, but have no doubt they regard us as far from being subdued, and are willing to treat rather than incur the preparations for what they conceive necessary for final success. An intelligent prisoner, Mr. Roulhac of Florida, recently returned, informs me that by the influence of his mercantile acquaintance, he was paroled and allowed to spend six weeks in the city of New-York, and to travel to Washington, etc. According to his observation, there is an abatement in the feelings of hostility to the South, and a disposition to peace, but upon the basis of reconstruction. Mr. Singleton of Illinois, who has been here at times for two or three weeks, and is a supposed *quasi* diplomat, but from the company he keeps is more of a speculator, gives the same account. The Virginia delegation in Congress, having in view the Secretary of State, declared a want of confidence in the cabinet, but struck no game except their own Secretary of War. He has resigned, and Breckinridge, it is announced, is to succeed him, ... a representative of a State which has not ten thousand men in our army. No reports are given from official sources of the fall of Fort Fisher. Private accounts represent it as a disgraceful affair. . . .

Mr. Trenholm insists on adding one hundred per cent to the taxes of last year, including tithes. He is a good merchant and has talent, but is not versed in the finances of a nation. General Lee has addressed a letter to a member of the Virginia Senate, advocating the enlistment of slaves as soldiers, with emancipation of themselves and families, and ultimately of the race. With such wild schemes and confessions of despair as this, it is high time to attempt peace, and I trust the commission above named may pave the way to it. . . .

Very faithfully yours,

W. A. GRAHAM.

RICHMOND, Feb. 5, 1865.

MY DEAR SIR: The commission to confer with the Northern Government returned yesterday evening. I have not seen any of the gentlemen, but learn on good authority that nothing was effected of a beneficial nature, except that a general exchange of prisoners on parole may be looked for. They were met on shipboard by Messrs. Lincoln and Seward in person, (in sight of Fortress Monroe,) who said they could entertain no proposition looking to the independence of the Southern States, and could only offer that these States should return to the Union under the Constitution in the existing condition of affairs, with slavery as it is, but liable to be abolished by an amendment of the Constitution. They brought also the information that Congress, on Wednesday last, had passed a bill, by a vote of one hundred and eighteen to fifty-four, to amend the Constitution, so as to abolish slavery in the States, which is to be submitted to the State Legislatures for approval of three fourths. These officers are said to have exhibited great courtesy and kindness in the interview, Lincoln recurring to what he had been willing to do in the outset, and from time to time since, but that public opinion now demanded his present ultimatum. The Commissioners saw large numbers of black troops on their journey. I have seen but few persons to-day ; but the impression will be that there is no alternative but to prosecute the war. The administration is weak in the estimation of Congress, and a vote of want of confidence could be carried through the Senate if approved by those it has been accustomed to consider Opposition. I am not sure that this vote will not be carried as to the Secretary of State. Senator Hill left yesterday for Georgia, to attend the session of the Legislature, and endeavor to revive public confidence, etc. The committee of our Legislature left the evening before the return of the Commissioners, disposed, I believe, to await further progress of events. The situation is critical, and requires a guidance beyond human ken.

Very truly yours.

RICHMOND, Feb. 12, 1865.

MY DEAR SIR : You will have seen in the papers the report of the Commissioners appointed to confer with the United States Government, with the message of the President, as well as his speech at the African Church, the addresses of the Secretary of State, and

of several members of Congress, at a public meeting
to give expression to sentiment on the result of the
mission.   Judging from these, and the editorials
of the newspapers of this city, there would appear
to be nothing in contemplation .but *bella, horrida
bella.* I was not present at any of these proceedings, but learn that the assemblages were large and
apparently very enthusiastic ; but no volunteers were
called for, nor any offered. Instead of that, labored
arguments were made in favor of making soldiers of
slaves.   The speech of the Secretary of State·went far
beyond the newspaper reports, and its imprudences in
his situation are the subject of severe criticism. He
declared among other things, " that unless the slaves
were armed, the cause was lost ;" with revelations of
details of the attempt at negotiation, exceedingly impolitic. All these demonstrations are likely to pass
off as the idle wind, and the great question still remains, What is to be done to save the country ?   Mr.
Stephens and Judge Campbell refused to make any
public addresses.   The former has gone home, and it
is understood does not design to speak in public there,
though the papers have announced the contrary. . . .
It seems they were under instructions not to treat except upon the basis of independence, and carried romantic propositions about an armistice, coupled with
an alliance to embark in a war with France, to maintain the Monroe doctrine, and expel Maximilian from
Mexico.   Lincoln was courteous and apparently anxious for a settlement ; but firm in the announcement
that nothing could be entertained till our difficulties

were adjusted, and that upon the basis of a restoration of the Union. That as far as he had power as President, amnesty, exemption from confiscation, etc., should be freely extended; reviewed his announcements in his inaugural, proclamations, messages, etc., to show what he considered his liberality to the South, and that he could unsay nothing that he had said. As to slavery, it must stand on the legislation of Congress, with the proposed amendments to the Constitution, which he informed them had passed both Houses, but which the dissent of ten States could still reject. These terms not being agreed to, he and Seward rose to depart, but with a manifestation of disappointment, as inferred by my informant, that propositions were not submitted on our side. Thus terminated the conference. There is a widening breach between the President and Congress; a growing opinion on their part that he is unequal to the present duties of his position, while there is a division of opinion as to the prospect of relief in a different line of policy and under different auspices. The military situation is threatening. Grant has been reënforced. Sherman seems to advance almost without impediment, and with divided counsels among our generals in that quarter, Judge Campbell thinks another mission should be sent; but regards it as out of the question in the temper and with the committals of the President. Our Legislature has adjourned; that of Georgia meets this week. *Speed in affairs is necessary*. There is not time for States to act in concert, (without which they can effect nothing,) nor sufficient harmony of views here for action without the executive; and many, perhaps a majority, are for the most desperate expedients. A short time will bring forth important results. I have written very freely, but in confidence that you would observe the proper secrecy. I would be glad to have any suggestions that may occur to you. Opportunities for consultation here are not so numerous as I could wish.

Very truly yours.

RICHMOND, Feb. 22, 1865.

MY DEAR SIR: . . . . . A bill to conscribe negroes in the army was postponed indefinitely in the Senate yesterday, in secret session. I *argued it* at length as unconstitutional according to the Dred Scott decision as well as inexpedient and dangerous. A bill for this purpose, which had passed the House, was laid on the table. There may be attempts to revive this fatal measure. All the influence of the administration and of General Lee was brought to bear, but without success. An effort is being made to instruct the Virginia senators to vote for it. Mr. Benjamin has been writing letters to induce the brigades of the army to declare for it. I rather regret that I did not join in a vote of want of confidence in him, which only failed. Had I gone for it, I learn it would have been carried by a considerable majority.

The military situation is exceedingly critical. There will be no stand made short of Greensboro; whether there successfully, is doubtful. . . . . . Opinion is growing in favor of more negotiations, to rescue the wreck of our affairs, if military results continue

adverse. I shall meet some friends this evening on
that topic. I write in haste. As to matters of confidence, please observe the proper secrecy. It is the
duty of the people to sustain the war till their authorities, Confederate or State, determine otherwise. But
in the mean time there is no reason for inflamed resolutions to do what may be found impossible, and which
they may be compelled to retract.

Very truly yours,
W. A. GRAHAM.

The publication of further extracts from these representative letters must be deferred to the succeeding
chapter. Meanwhile the thoughtful student of the
events of that day will recognize the direct hand of
Providence in the continuation of the war till the utter
failure of our resources was so fully manifest that
peace, when it came, should be *unchallenged*, *profound*,
and *universal*.

CHAPTER IX.

STATE OF PARTIES — THE FEELING OF THE PEOPLE — THE
"PEACE" PARTY—IMPORTANT LETTER FROM GOVERNOR VANCE
IN JANUARY, 1864—HIS REËLECTION—THE WAR PARTY—
THE PEACE PARTY—THE MODERATES—GOVERNOR GRAHAM'S
LETTER OF MARCH, 1865—EVACUATION OF RICHMOND.

HE who would write a history of public events
passing in his own day will find, among the many
obstacles in the way of a clear and correct delineation,
that he is continually met with doubts and hesitations
in his own mind as to the impartiality of his views
and decisions. The prejudices of party feeling must
inevitably confuse and blind to some extent even the
clearest judgment; and while a consciousness of this
renders the faithful historian doubly anxious to exercise strict impartiality, he will find himself embarrassed
by the divisions and subdivisions of opinion, bewildered
by conflicting representations, and in danger of becoming involved in contradictions and inconsistencies.
In the first chapter of these sketches it was remarked,
with reference to the North and the South, that there
was too much to be forgotten and too much to be forgiven between them, to hope at present for a fair and
unprejudiced history of the war on either side. In re-

lation to the parties that existed among ourselves during the war, it is equally true that the time has not yet arrived for a fair statement or comparison of their respective merits or demerits. While there is much that may be written and much that has been written which may with propriety be given to the public, there is much more that must at present be suppressed or receive only a passing notice. More especially is this true in regard to the secession party and its adherents. Yet in presenting even these slight sketches of the state of things during the war in North-Carolina, it would be impossible to ignore them, and unfair to represent them as without influence among us. For while it is incontestably true that the great mass of our people engaged reluctantly in the war, and hailed the prospect of peace and an honorable reünion, yet there was at the same time hardly a town in the State or an educated and refined community which did not furnish their quota of those who, without having been *original secessionists*, yet had thrown themselves with extreme ardor on the side of the Southern States rights, and were ready to go all lengths in support of the war, and who are even now, though helpless and powerless, unwilling to admit that they were either in the wrong or in the minority. With many of them it was the triumph of heroic sentiment and generous feeling over the calmer suggestions of reason, for they were chiefly among our most refined and highly cultivated citizens. As a party, if not numerous, they were well organized and compact; they were socially and politically conspicuous, and did most of the writing and talking. They differed from the great body of their fellow-citizens, chiefly in the intensity of their loyalty toward President Davis and his government—being resolved to support him at all hazards—and in the implacable temper they manifested toward the common enemy. One who mingled freely with both parties, and by turns sympathized with both, and who would fain do justice to both, will find it impossible to adjust their conflicting representations, and at the same time observe the prudent reticence which our present circumstances imperatively demand. Two of the most prominent and influential leaders of the war party, Governors Ellis and Winslow, have passed beyond the reach of earthly tribunals, and of the living actors it is obvious that no mention can now be made, Very different but no less cogent reasons impose a similar reticence in relation to the more numerous but not more respectable or influential organization known as the "Peace Party" of the last eighteen months of the war, and as "Union men of the straitest sect" at this day. Of this party, Governor Holden is the admitted founder and the present head, and Senator Pool his most prominent exponent. A representation of their principles and their history should be made by themselves. They possess all the materials and all the abilities requisite for the work, and they owe it to themselves and to the public to place it on record for the judgment of their cotemporaries and of posterity. They and they alone are competent to the performance of this duty in the best manner. The precise date of the earliest formation of this party is given in the following letter from Governor Vance, which is inserted here, not only as affording a clear view of the principles which guided *his* course of action, but as enabling the reader to comprehend Governor Graham's policy, exhibited in the further extracts from his correspondence.

This letter was addressed by Governor Vance to the same friend who received the letter given in my first number, and is marked by the same clearness and energy of thought, the same generosity of feeling, and the same unaffected ardor of patriotism which characterize all of the Governor's letters that I have been privileged to see.

RALEIGH, January 2, 1864.

MY DEAR SIR: The final plunge which I have been dreading and avoiding—that is to separate me from a large number of my political friends, is about to be made. It is now a fixed policy of Mr. Holden and others to call a convention in May to take North-Carolina back to the United States, and the agitation has already begun. Resolutions advocating this course were prepared a few days ago in the *Standard* office, and sent to Johnson county to be passed at a public meeting next week; and a series of meetings are to be held all over the State.

For any cause now existing, or likely to exist, I can never consent to this course.

Never. But should it be inevitable, and I be unable to prevent it, as I have no right to suppose I could, believing that it would be ruinous alike to the State and the Confederacy, producing war and devastation at home, and that it would steep the name of North-Carolina in infamy, and make her memory a reproach among the nations, it is my determination quietly to retire to the army and find a death which will enable my children to say that their father was not consenting to their degradation.   This may sound a little wild and romantic—to use no stronger expression—but it is for your eye only.   I feel, sir, in many respects, as a son toward you; and when the many acts of kindness I have received at your hands are remembered, and the parental interest you have always manifested for my welfare, the feeling is not unnatural.   I therefore approach you frankly in this matter.

I will not present the arguments against the proposed proceeding.   There is something to be said on both sides.   We are sadly pushed to the wall by the enemy on every side, it is true.   That can be answered by military men and a reference to history.   Many people have been worse off, infinitely, and yet triumphed.   Our finances and other material resources are not in worse condition than were those of our fathers in 1780–'81, though repudiation is inevitable. Almost every argument against the chances of our success can be answered but one; that is the cries of women and little children for bread !   Of all others, that is the hardest for a man of humane sentiments to meet, especially when the sufferers rejoin to your appeals to their patriotism, "You, Governor, have plenty; your children have never felt want."   Still, no great political or moral blessing ever has been or can be attained without suffering.   Such is our moral constitution, that liberty and independence can only be gathered of blood and misery, sustained and fostered by devoted patriotism and heroic manhood. This requires a deep hold on the popular heart; and whether our people are willing to pay this price for Southern independence, I am somewhat inclined to doubt. But, sir, in tracing the sad story of the backing down, the self-imposed degradation of a great people, the historian shall not say it was due to the weakness of their Governor, and that Saul was consenting unto their death! Neither do I desire, for the sake of a sentiment, to involve others in a ruin which they might avoid by following more ignoble counsels. As God liveth, there is nothing which I would not do or dare for the people who so far beyond my deserts have honored me. But in resisting this attempt to lead them back, humbled and degraded, to the arms of their enemies, who have slaughtered their sons, outraged their daughters, and wasted their fields with fire, and lay them bound at the feet of a master who promises them *only life*, provided they will swear to uphold his administration, and surrender to the hangman those whom they themselves placed in the position which constitutes their crime—in resisting this, I say, I feel that I am serving them truly, worthily.

In approaching this, the crisis of North-Carolina's fate, certainly of my own career, I could think of no one to whom I could more appropriately go for advice than yourself for the reasons before stated. If you can say any thing to throw light on my path, or enable me to avoid the rocks before me, I shall be thankful. My great anxiety now, as I can scarcely hope to avert the contemplated action of the State, is to prevent civil war, and to preserve life and property as far as may be possible. With due consideration on the part of public men, which I fear is not to be looked for, this might be avoided. It shall be my aim, under God, at all events.

All the circumstances considered, do you think I ought again to be a candidate? It is a long time to the election, it is true, but the issue will be upon the country by spring. My inclination is to take the stump early, and spend all my time and strength in trying to warm and harmonize the people.

. . . .

Believe me, my dear sir, yours sincerely,

Z. B. VANCE.

Governor Vance, it is well known, took the field against this new party; and in the overwhelming majority with which he was reëlected the following summer, convincing proof was given that much as North-Carolinians desired peace, they were not willing to take irregular or revolutionary measures to obtain it, and that they preferred even a hopeless war to a dishonorable reünion.

Besides the Moderates, who constituted the bulk of the people, and the War Party, and the "Peace Party," there were many besides of a class which can never be influential, but may well be counted among the *impedimenta* of all great movements; who, unable to answer the arguments of either side, could give no counsel to either, though they were always prepared to blame any unsuccessful movement made in any direction. These, overwhelmed by doubts and fears in the moment of peril, could only wring their hands in hopeless inefficiency. Surrounded with such conflicting elements, those who fain would have led the people " by a right way," found the obstacles interposed by party spirit almost insurmountable. In presenting Governor Graham, therefore, as a representative North-Carolinian, it must be borne in mind that there were many men among us true and patriotic, but so ardently devoted to the cause of the Confederacy as to remain to the last implacable toward any attempt at negotiation, who looked upon all suggestions tending that way as dastardly and traitorous to the South, and who, backed by the whole civil and military Confederate authorities, were ready to brand and arrest as traitors the authors of any such move.

With these reflections, I resume the extracts from Governor Graham's correspondence, assured that his inaction in the momentous crisis, deprecated as it was at the time, by one party as evincing too little energy in behalf of peace, if not a disposition to continue the war; and reviled by the other as indicative of a disposition toward inglorious surrender and reconstruction, was in effect *masterly*, that masterly inactivity with which he who surveys the tumult of conflict from an eminence, may foresee and calmly await the approaching and inevitable end.

RICHMOND, March 12, 1865.

MY DEAR SIR: The passing week will develop important events. The President has requested Congress to prolong its session to receive communications which he desires to make. Three days have since elapsed, but nothing but routine messages have thus far been received. I am not at liberty to anticipate what is coming, or probably to reveal it when received; but doubtless the whole horizon of the situation will be surveyed, and an occasion presented for determinate action as to the future. In my opinion, he is powerless, and can neither make peace for our security nor war with success. But *nous verrons.*

The bill to arm slaves has become a law. It professes to take them only with the consent of their masters; and in the event of failure in this, to call on the State authorities to furnish. I trust no master in North-Carolina will volunteer or consent to begin this process of abolition, as I feel very confident the General Assembly will not.

We hear the enemy are near Fayetteville, notwithstanding the check to Kilpatrick by Hampton. I think our officers of state, except the Governor, should not leave Raleigh, but should claim protection for the State property from fire or other destruction, if the enemy come there. A raid of Sheridan's force has been above this city some days, destroying the James River Canal and other property; and last night, at one A.M., the alarm-bell was rung, calling out the local force for the defense of the city, it being reported that the enemy was within seven miles. It is said to-day that the party has joined Grant below Richmond. Commander Hollins and several citizens are said to have been killed by them.

You may conceive that the path of those intrusted with the great interests of the people is beset with difficulties ; but it must be trodden with what serenity and wisdom we may command.

Very truly yours,   W. A. GRAHAM.

HILLSBORO, N. C., March 26, 1865.

MY DEAR SIR : I am much indebted for your note by Dr. H——. I arrived at home on this day week, and the next day went to Raleigh to have an interview with the Governor on the subject-matter referred to in your letter. The result was a convocation of the Council of State to assemble to-morrow. The Legislature of Virginia has taken a recess until the twenty-ninth instant, and I think it very important that that of North-Carolina shall be in session as early thereafter as possible. The war is now nearly reduced to a contest between these two States and the United States. The military situation is by no means favorable, and I perceive no solution of our difficulties except through the action of the States. The public men in the service of the Confederacy are so trammeled by the parts they have borne in past events, and their apprehensions as to a consistent record, that the government does not answer the present necessities of the country. I wish, if possible, to see you in the course of this week for a full conference on these important topics. The Governor is, I think, reasonable, but was much surprised by some of the facts I communicated to him. I do not know the disposition of the Council. If the Legislature shall be convened, I will attend their session, and if desired, will address them in private meeting. Much pertaining to the present position of affairs can not with propriety be communicated to the public.

I received last night a telegram from my son James, informing me that his brothers John and Robert were both wounded—the former in both legs, the latter in the left, in an attack by General Lee on the left of Grant's line yesterday morning. I am expecting another message to-night from General Ransom, which may occasion me to go to Petersburg to attend to them. Lee was successful in surprising the enemy and driving him from three lines of intrenchments and taking five hundred prisoners; but by a concentrated fire of the artillery of the foe, was compelled to retire. James says he was unhurt.

I am also under a great necessity to go to the Catawba, but with a large force of *reserve artillery* all around us, and some apprehensions of the advance of Sherman, I know not which way to turn.

I had a conversation with Governor Morehead at Greensboro, and believe he realizes the situation.

Very sincerely yours, W. A. GRAHAM.

If the Legislature of Virginia convened at Richmond on the twenty-ninth of March, 1865, small time was allowed for their deliberations; and it would have been of very little practical utility if the General Assembly of North-Carolina had been summoned to correspond with it at that date. On the second of April, Richmond was evacuated. Our President and his cabinet were fugitives in the clear starlight of that woful night; our capital was delivered over to a mob, and in flames. But we did not even dream of it. It was more than a week before the certain intelligence was received in Central Carolina, and even then many doubted. Dismal rumors from Lee's army, of the fall of Petersburg, of the fate of Richmond, were whispered, but were contradicted every hour by those whose wish was father to the thought that there was hope yet, that all was not lost. We were indeed in the very turning-point and fatal crisis of the great *Southern States rights struggle;* but we hardly realized through what an era of history we were living. In the quiet and secluded village in which I now write, the uninterrupted order of our daily life afforded a strong confirmation of the great English historian's saying, that in all wars, after all, but a comparatively small portion of a nation are actually engaged or affected. The children plan their little fishing-parties, the plow-boy whistles in the field, the wedding-supper is provided, and the daily course of external domestic life in general flows as smoothly as ever, except immediately in the track of the armies. It is not indifference nor insensibility. It is the wise and beneficent order of Providence that it should be with the body politic as with our physical frame. One part may suffer mutilation, and though a sympathetic thrill of anguish pervade every nerve of the whole body, yet the natural functions are not suspended in any other member. Men must lie down, and sleep, and eat, and go through the ordinary rou-

tine of daily duty in circumstances of the most tragic
interest. It is only on the stage that they tear their
hair and lie prostrate on the ground. So we still exchanged our Confederate money with each other—the
bright, new, clean twenties and tens, which we tried
to believe were worth something, for there was still a
faint magical aroma of value hovering round those
promises to pay " six months after a treaty of peace
with the United States;" $25 a yard for country
jeans, $30 a yard for calico, $10 for a pair of cotton
socks, $20 for a wheat-straw hat, $25 for a bushel of
meal, and $10 to have a tooth pulled, and very cheap
at that — if we had only known all. Mothers were
still preparing boxes for their boys in the army ; the
farmer got his old battered tools in readiness for his
spring's work ; the merchant went daily to preside
over the scanty store of thread, needles, and buttons,
remnants of calico, and piles of homespun, which now
constituted his stock in trade ; and our little girls still
held their regular meetings for knitting soldiers'
socks, all unconscious of the final crash so near, while
the peach-trees were all abloom and spring was putting on all her bravery.

CHAPTER X.

WHEN the intention of General Johnston to uncover the city of Raleigh became generally known, and when the retrograde movement of his army commenced in the direction of Chapel Hill, and along the line of the Central Railroad; when General Wheeler's troopers, followed hard by Kilpatrick's command, poured along our country roads, and the people gave half of their provision to the retreating friends, and were stripped of the other half by the advancing foe; there were few thoughtful persons in Orange county whose waking and sleeping hours were not perturbed and restless.

What could be done? Whither were we tending? What was to be the result? An hour or two of anxious reflection on such questions before day on the morning of April 8th, induced Governor Swain, President of the University of North Carolina—than whom, though immured in the cloisters of a venerable literary Institution, no man in the Confederacy took a keener interest in the progress of public events, surveyed the action of parties with more sagacious apprehension, or was oftener consulted by leading men— induced him to rise at an early hour and make another effort to influence the public authorities of the State to adopt immediate measures for saving what remained of the country from devastation, and the seat of government and the University from the conflagration which had overwhelmed the capitals of our sister States. He wrote the subjoined letter to Governor Graham, at daylight; but such was the apprehension of the time, that it was difficult to find a messenger, and still more difficult to procure a horse to bear it from the University to Hillsboro. By ten that morning it was on the way, and by six in the evening Governor Graham's reply was received.

CHAPEL HILL, }
Saturday Morning, April 8, 1865. }

MY DEAR SIR : Since the organization of the State government, in December, 1776, North-Carolina has never passed through so severe an ordeal as that we are now undergoing. Unless something can be done to prevent it, suffering and privation, and death— death in the battle-field, and death in the most horrible of all forms, the slow and lingering death of famine, are imminent to thousands, not merely men, but women and children.

The General Assembly, by its own resolution, is not to meet until the 16th of May. If the Governor shall desire to convene the members at an earlier day, it may not, in the present state of the country, be possible to effect his purpose. Some of the members will find it impossible to reach Raleigh in the existing state of the railroads, others may be in danger of arrest if they shall attempt it in any way, and there are few who can leave home without peril to person or property. We are compelled, then, to look to other sources for relief from the dangers by which we are environed. In ancient times, when the most renowned of republics experienced similar trials, the decree went forth :

" *Viderent consules ne quid detrimenti respublica caperet.*"

A dictatorship is, in my opinion, repugnant to every principle of civil liberty, and I would neither propose nor support one under any existing circumstances. But something must be done, and done immediately, or the opening campaign will be brief and fatal. Anarchy may ensue, and from anarchy the descent to a military despotism is speedy and natural.

The State has no such citizen to whom all eyes turn with deep anxiety and confident hope for the counsel and guidance demanded by the crisis, as yourself. Fully satisfied of this fact, I venture to suggest the propriety of your meeting me in Raleigh on Monday morning, and inviting a conference with the Governor on the state of public affairs. He numbers among his many friends none who have yielded him earlier, more constant, or more zealous support, in the trying circumstances in which Providence has been pleased to place him, than ourselves. I am the oldest of his predecessors in his office, and about the time of your entrance into public life, was summoned to the discharge of similar duties in the midst of similar perils. I have had from him too numerous and decided proofs of confidence, respect, and affection, to doubt that he will listen to me kindly ; and I know that he will receive you with as great cordiality and give as favorable consideration to your suggestions as he would yield to any citizen or functionary in the Confederacy. Perhaps he may be disposed not only to hear us, but to invite all his predecessors—Morehead, Manly, Reid, Bragg, and Clark—to unite with us in consultation at a time and under circumstances calling for the exercise of the highest powers of statesmanship. At present, I do not deem it incumbent on me, even if my views were more fully matured, to intimate the ideas I entertain of what must be done, and done promptly, to arrest the downward tendency of public affairs.

I content myself with simply urging that you shall meet me in Raleigh, as above proposed, on Monday, if it be possible, and if you concur with me in opinion that we are in the midst of imminent perils.

Yours very sincerely,

D. L. SWAIN.

HILLSBORO, April 8, 1865.

MY DEAR SIR: Yours of this date has just been received, and I entirely concur in your estimate of the dangers that environ us.

I left Richmond thoroughly convinced that—

1st. Independence for the Southern Confederacy was perfectly hopeless.

2d. That through the administration of Mr. Davis we could expect no peace, so long as he shall be supplied with the resources of war; and that

3d. It was the duty of the State government immediately to move for the purpose of effecting an adjustment of the quarrel with the United States.

I accordingly remained at home but twenty-four hours (that being the Sabbath, and having had no sleep the night preceding) before repairing to Raleigh to lay before the Governor such information as I possessed, and to urge him to convene the General Assembly immediately. I told him that Richmond would fall in less than thirty days, and would be followed probably by a rout or dispersion of Lee's army for want of food, if for no other cause. That the Confederate Government had no plan or policy beyond this event, although it was generally anticipated. That I had reason to believe that General Lee was anxious for an accommodation. That Johnston had not and could not raise a sufficient force to encounter Sherman. That I had conferred with the President, and found him, though in an anxious frame of mind, constrained by the scruple that he could not " commit suicide " by treating his Government out of existence, nor even ascertain for the States what terms would be yielded, provided they consented to reädopt the Constitution of the United States. That the wisest and best men with whom I had been associated, or had conversed, were anxious for a settlement; but were so trammeled by former committals, and a false pride, or other like causes, that they were unable to move themselves, or in their States, but were anxious that others should ; and that it was now the case of a beleaguered garrison before a superior force, considering the question whether it was best to capitulate on terms, or hold out to be put to the sword on a false point of honor.

The Governor was evidently surprised by my statement of facts, and, I apprehend, incredulous at least as to my conclusions. He agreed to consider the subject, and to convene the council on that day week. I heard nothing of their action, and being solicitous on the subject, on Thursday last I visited Raleigh again, found the Governor on the cars here returning from Statesville, and we journeyed together, and I dined with him after arrival. He said he had purposed visiting me, but it had been neglected ; that a bare *quorum* of his council attended the meeting, and being equally divided, he had not summoned the Legislature ; but that Mr. Gilmer, whom I had advised him to consult, and every body else now he believed agreed with me in opinion. He had recently seen Mr. Gilmer, and he suggested to him to solicit an interview with General Sherman on the subject of peace. I told him that President Davis would probably complain of this, and should be apprised of it if held. He replied that this of course should be done. I suggested, however, that even if this course were taken, he should be in a position to act independently of the President, and therefore should convene the General Assembly. On this he was reluctant, but finally agreed to call the Council of State again. I told him in parting, that if, in any event, he supposed I could be useful to him, to notify me, and I would attend him. I am induced to believe that the result of the deliberation of the council was not disagreeable to him; but since the fall of Richmond he has a truer conception of the situation. I wrote him a note on the day the council met, advising him of your concurrence in the necessity of calling the General Assembly. He went, on Friday last, to witness a review of Johnston's army, and proposed to me to accompany him. I declined; not seeing any good to be accomplished there. General Johnston I know, and appreciate him highly.

. . . .

I hope you will go, as you propose, to see Governor Vance. I thought of inviting you to my first interview with him; and if he shall contrive a meeting with Sherman, I hope you may be present. I do not think it necessary, perhaps not advisable myself, to visit him again on these topics. My conversations with him were very full and earnest. I told him I should attend the session of the General Assembly, and if desired would address them in secret session; that I had had confidential conversations with a committee of the Virginia Legislature, which had taken a recess for ten days, and that it was important to act in concert with that body; that my colleagues in the House, the Leaches, Turner, Ramsay, Fuller, and Logan, were ready to call a session of the Assembly together by advertisement; but all this had no effect in procuring a recommendation to the council in favor of the call.

.   .   .   .

I do not perceive that any thing will be gained by a convention of those who have held the office of chief magistrate. . . . *Prejudices are still rife,* and the poison of party spirit yet lurks in the sentiments of many otherwise good men, who swear by the Administration, and will wage indefinite war while other people can be found to fight it.

Süppose you come to my house to-morrow, and take the cars from here next morning. There is much to say that I can not write. I set off to Chapel Hill this morning to see you; but riding first to the dépôt to inquire for news, thought I had intelligence of my sons in the army. This proved a mistake, but prevented my visit. I fear that John and Robert and my servant Davy fell into the enemy's hands on the evacuation of Petersburg. They were at the house of William R. Johnson, Jr., and doing well. Cooke's brigade, in which James is a captain, was hotly engaged in the action of Sunday. I have no tidings of his fate. Hoping to see you soon, I remain, yours very truly,   W. A. GRAHAM.

Governor Swain, in compliance with Governor Graham's request that he would take Hillsboro in his way to Raleigh, spent the next day at his house in Hillsboro, in consultation as to the best mode of effecting their common purpose. They agreed upon the course of action indicated in the following outline drawn up by Governor Graham :

MY DEAR SIR : Referring to our conversation in relation to the critical and urgent condition of our affairs as regards the public enemy, I am of opinion that—

1st. The General Assembly should be convened at the earliest day practicable.

2d. That when convened, it should pass resolutions expressive of a desire for opening negotiations for peace, and stopping the effusion of blood ; and inviting the other States of the South to unite in the movement.

3d. That to effect this object, it should elect commissioners to treat with the Government of the United States, and report the result to a convention, which should be at once called by the Legislature to wield the sovereign power of the State in any emergency that may arise out of the changing state of events.

4th. That in the event of Sherman's advance upon the capital, or indeed without that event, let the Governor propose a conference, or send a commission to treat with him for a suspension of hostilities, until the further action of the State shall be ascertained in regard to the termination of the war.

All this I should base upon the doctrine of the President of the Confederate States, that he conceives it inconsistent with his duty to entertain negotiations for peace except upon the condition of absolute independence to the Southern Confederacy, with all the territories claimed as belonging to each State comprising it, and should give him the earliest information of the proceedings in progress.

Very truly yours,   W. A. GRAHAM.

April 9, 1865.

At seven the next (Monday) morning, Governor Swain took the train from Hillsboro to Raleigh, dined with Governor Vance and at the close of a long and earnest conference, the latter agreed to carry out the scheme submitted if the concurrence of General Johnston could be obtained. He promised to ride out immediately to General Johnston's headquarters and consult him upon the subject. The next morning he authorized Governor Swain to telegraph Governor Graham and request his presence. The latter responded promptly that he would come down in the eleven o'clock train that night, and Governor Swain spent the night with Governor Vance in anxious expectation of his arrival. The train failed to arrive until three o'clock on Wednesday morning. Governor Swain, at early dawn, found Governor Vance writing dispatches by candle-light, and Governor Graham was at the door before sunrise. Mrs. Vance and her children had retired from Raleigh to a place of supposed greater safety, and the three gentlemen, together with Colonel Burr, of Governor Vance's staff, were the only occupants of the executive mansion. After an early breakfast, they went to the capitol, where a communication from Governor Vance to General Sherman was prepared. General Johnston, in the mean time, had retired in the direction of Hillsboro, and General Hardee was the officer of highest grade then in Raleigh. He promptly accepted an invitation from Governor Vance to be present at a conference, prepared a safe-conduct through his lines for Governors Swain and Graham, who undertook the commission to General Sherman ; and by ten o'clock, attended by three of the Governor's staff—Surgeon-General Warren, Colonel Burr, and Major Devereux—they left Raleigh in a special train, bearing a flag of truce, for General Sherman's headquarters. Governor Bragg, Mr. Moore, and Mr. Raynor had all been consulted in relation to the course proposed to be pursued, and all had concurred most heartily in its propriety and necessity. There were others who were not consulted, who nevertheless suspected the design of those concerned in these conferences ; and one of them is understood to have kept President Davis, who was then in Greensboro, regularly advised by telegraph of all, and more than all, that was contemplated by the embassy.

The fate of the mission, and its final results, form, as I doubt not my readers will agree, as interesting and important a chapter in the history of the State as has occurred since its organization.

CHAPTER XI.

THE commissioners to General Sherman from Governor Vance left Raleigh on Wednesday morning,
April twelfth, at ten o'clock, as before stated. They
were expected to return by four o'clock that afternoon, at the farthest, as General Sherman was understood to be not more than fourteen miles from the
city.

That day Raleigh presented, perhaps, less external
appearance of terror and confusion than might have
been supposed. That General Sherman would arrive
there in the course of his march, had been anticipated
ever since his entrance into the State; and General
Johnston, on the tenth, had given Governor Vance
notice of his intention to uncover the city, so that

such preparations as could be made to meet their fate had been completed. An immense amount of State property had been removed to various points along the Central Railroad. Some forty thousand blankets, overcoats, clothes, and English cloth equal to at least one hundred thousand suits complete; leather and shoes equal to ten thousand pairs; great quantities of cotton cloth and yarns, and cotton-cards; six thousand scythe-blades; one hundred and fifty thousand pounds of bacon; forty thousand bushels of corn; a very large stock of imported medical stores; and many other articles of great value, together with the public records, Treasury and Literary Board, and other effects, were mostly deposited at Graham, Greensboro, and Salisbury. Governor Vance and the State officers under his direction had worked day and night, with indefatigable zeal, to effect this transportation, so that before mid-day on the twelfth every thing was in readiness. Every suggestion of ingenuity, meanwhile, had been put in practice by the citizens in concealing their private property, though, indeed, with very little hope that they would escape such accomplished and practiced marauders as those who composed the approaching "grand army." Men who had been on the *qui vive*, ever since leaving Atlanta, to discover and appropriate or wantonly destroy all of household treasures and valuables that lay in their way, or anywhere within sixty miles of their way, snappers-up of even such unconsidered trifles as an old negro's silver watch or a baby's corals—from the hands of such as these what was to be expected; what nook, or cranny, or foot of inclosed ground would be safe from their search! Many citizens repaired to Governor Vance's office for advice and comfort, and none left him without greater courage to meet what was coming. Though overburdened with cares and unspeakable anxieties on this memorable day, all found him easy of access and ready to give prudent counsel to those who asked for it. He advised the citizens generally to remain quiet in their own houses, and, as far as possible, protect their families by their presence. He himself was resolved to await the return of the embassy to Sherman, and learn upon what conditions he could remain and exercise the functions of his office, or if at all.

When the train bearing the commissioners reached General Hampton's lines, they requested an interview with him. The safe-conduct from General Hardee, and the letter from Governor Vance to General Sherman were shown him. He remarked that General Hardee was his superior, and that of course he yielded to authority, but expressed his own doubts of the propriety or expediency of the mission. He prepared a dispatch, however, immediately, and transmitted it by a courier to General Sherman, together with a note from Governors Graham and Swain, requesting to be advised of the time and place at which a conference might take place.

General Hardee then retired with his staff, and the train moved slowly on. When at the distance, perhaps, of two miles, one of his couriers dashed up, halted the train, and informed the commissioners that he was directed by General Hampton to say that he had just received an order from General Johnston to with-draw their safe conduct, and direct them to return to Raleigh. They directed the courier to return and say to the General that such an order ought to be given personally or in writing, and that the train would be stationary till he could be heard from. This message was replied to by the prompt appearance of the Gen-eral himself. The extreme courtesy of his manner, and his air and bearing confirmed the impression made in the previous interview, that he was a frank, and gallant, and chivalrous soldier. He read the copy of a dispatch that he had sent by a courier to General Sherman, which in substance was as follows:

"GENERAL: Since my dispatch of half an hour ago, circumstances have occurred which induce me to give you no further trouble in relation to the mission of ex-Governors Graham and Swain. These gentlemen will return with the flag of truce to Raleigh."

This dispatch he had sent immediately on receiving General Johnston's order to direct their return. The commissioners were of course surprised and disap-pointed. The mission was not entered upon without the deliberate assent and advice of General Johnston, after a full consultation with Governor Vance, and also with General Hardee's entire concurrence, and a safe-conduct from him in General Johnston's absence. The engine, however, was reversed, General Hamp-ton retired, and the train had proceeded slowly about a mile or so in the direction of Raleigh, when it was again halted, and this time by a detachment of a hundred Spencer rifles, a portion of Kilpatrick's cavalry, under the command of General Atkins. The commissioners were informed that they must proceed to the headquarters of General Kilpatrick, distant a mile or more. While waiting for a conveyance they were courteously treated, and a band of music ordered up for their entertainment. After a brief interval General Kilpatrick's carriage arrived for them, and they proceeded in it under escort to the residence of Mr. Fort, where the General then was. He received them politely, examined the safe-conduct of General Hardee, and the dispatches for General Sherman, and then remarked that the circumstances in which they were placed, according to the laws of war, gave him the right, which, however, he had not the smallest intention of exercising, to consider them as prisoners of war.

"It is true, gentlemen," said he, "that you came under the protection of a flag of truce, and are the bearers of important dispatches from your Governor to my Commanding General, but that gave you no right to cross my skirmish-line while a fight was going on."

Governor Graham remarked that the circumstances under which they came explained themselves, and were their own justification. That in a special train, with open windows, proceeding with the deliberation proper to a flag of truce, with only five persons in a single car, they had little temptation to proceed if they had known, in time to stop, that they were to be exposed to a cross-fire from the skirmish-lines of the two armies.

General Kilpatrick replied that all that was very true, but that it was proper, nevertheless, that he should require them to proceed to General Sherman's headquarters. He then remarked that the war was virtually at an end, and that every man who voluntarily shed blood from that time forth, would be a murderer; and read a general order from General Sherman, congratulating the army on the surrender of General Lee, intelligence of which had just reached him by telegraph. This was the first intimation our commissioners had received of this final blow to the Southern cause. It was indeed not unexpected, but no anticipation of such tidings can equal the moment of realization.; and to receive it under such circumstances, where extreme caution and self-command were an imperative duty, and where no expression could be allowed to the natural feelings of anguish and dismay with which it filled their breasts, gave an additional pang.

General Kilpatrick further stated, among other things, that the course pursued by General Lee was illustrative of the importance of regular military training; that an able and skillful commander knew when to fight, and when it was a more imperative duty to surrender; that a brave but rash and inexperienced officer would have sacrificed his army, and involved the whole country in ruin for the want of the proper skill to direct, and the *prestige* to sustain him in the discharge of a duty requiring more than courage.

After an hour or two's delay, the commissioners were escorted back to the train which was in waiting where they had left it, and thence proceeded to General Sherman's headquarters, passing for several miles through open columns of large bodies of troops, amidst the deafening cheers with which they welcomed the surrender of the great Confederate commander, and the arrival of a commission which, as they supposed, was authorized to treat for the surrender of General Johnston's army.

General Sherman, attended by his aids, met the commission at the station-house at Clayton, and conducted them to his tent. Governor Graham presented the letter from Governor Vance, and entered into a discussion of the various points it embraced, and found General Sherman apparently desirous to accede to its propositions as far as was possible for him, and ready to make an amicable and generous arrangement with the State government.

I have endeavored to procure copies of all the official letters written by Governor Vance at this important crisis in our affairs, but, with one exception, have failed. Copies of these letters, together with his letter-book then in use, with other important documents, were packed in a box which was captured at Greensboro, and taken to Washington City, as I have elsewhere mentioned. These records will doubtless be restored to the State at no distant day; and our people will yet have proof that their Governor did all that man could do—I may say all that a man thwarted by undue interference could do—to save the State and her capital from outrage, and humiliation, and anarchy.

I subjoin General Sherman's reply to the letter delivered by the commission:

HEADQUARTERS MILITARY DIVISION
OF THE MISSISSIPPI, IN THE FIELD,
GULLY'S STATION, N. C., April 12, 1865.

To his Excellency Z. B. Vance, Governor of the State of North-Carolina:

SIR: I have the honor to acknowledge the receipt of your communication of this date, and inclose you a safeguard for yourself and any members of the State government that choose to remain in Raleigh. I would gladly have enabled you to meet me here, but some interruption occurred to the train by the orders of General Johnston, after it had passed within the lines of my cavalry advance; but as it came out of Raleigh in good faith, it shall return in good faith, and will in no measure be claimed by us.

I doubt if hostilitie scan be suspended as between the army of the Confederate government and the one I command; but I will aid you all in my power to contribute to the end you aim to reach—the termination of the existing war.

I am, truly, your obedient servant,

W. T. SHERMAN,
Major-General.

In however unfavorable a light strict regard for the truth of history places General Sherman as a disciplinarian and leader of the great army that swept the Southern States with a besom of destruction; however dark the pictures of lawless pillage and brutal outrage, unrestrained and uncensured by the Commanding General—if indeed they were not especially directed and approved by him and his officers; however unenviable General Sherman's fame in *these* respects, equal regard for truth demands that in representing him at the council-board he shall appear in a much more commendable aspect, exhibiting there feelings of humanity and a capacity for enlarged and generous statesmanship entirely worthy of a really great general. If General Sherman's views and plans for closing the war had been adopted by his government, there can be no doubt that peace would have been *accomplished* in less than two months from the surrender of our armies; peace that would have been speedily followed by good-will in every Southern State, in spite of the waste and burning track of his army.

The hope which the commissioners had entertained of being able to return to Raleigh on the evening of the same day, was now found to be impracticable, owing to the various delays and impediments they had met with. General Sherman promised that their detention should be as brief as possible; but it soon became obvious that he intended they should spend the night at his headquarters. He had been promptly advised of General Hampton's having required their return to Raleigh, and had taken the necessary measures to prevent it, and was now equally determined that nothing should thwart the beneficial results of their conference, or any advantage that might accrue therefrom. The gentlemen were in his power, and submitted to his requisitions quietly, not cheerfully. It was intimated to them that the engine which brought them down required some repairs, and so soon as this could be effected, the train should again be at their service. The reply to Governor Vance's letter was placed in their hands, and a safe-conduct and permission to proceed in the train to Hillsboro, after the necessary interview with Governor Vance. General Sherman hoped they might be able to get off by midnight; but if that should be found impossible, they might retire to rest, take a cup of coffee with him at daylight, and breakfast in Raleigh. A couple of hours were spent in general conversation on public affairs, and less exciting topics.

At the close of the official conference between Governor Graham and General Sherman, Governor Swain remarked to the latter that, at the beginning of their troubles they were engaged in kindred pursuits. "Yes, sir," said the General. "I am aware that you are the President of the University of North-Carolina; and I was the Superintendent of the State Military Academy of Louisiana." "Two or three of your boys," said the Governor, "were with me for a time." "Yes," replied the General, "and many more of yours have been with me during the war, who came, poor fellows, before they were men, and when they ought to have remained with you; and they too frequently helped to fill my hospitals. I think, however, when they return, they will do me the justice to tell you that I treated them kindly." Governor Swain inquired for General Blair, remarking that he was his pupil in 1837. General Sherman replied that he was only two hours in the rear, and that he had just been reading terrible accounts in a Raleigh paper of his proceedings in Fayetteville, adding, "I will turn Frank over to you to answer for it in the morning." In connection with this, reference was made to the burning of Columbia. The General remarked with great emphasis : "I have been grossly misrepresented in regard to Columbia. I changed my headquarters eight times during that night, and with every general officer under my command, strained every nerve to stop the fire. I declare in the presence of my God that Hampton burned Columbia, and that he alone is responsible for it. He collected immense piles of cotton in the streets and set them on fire ; the wind rose during the night, and dispersed the flakes of burning cotton among the shingle-roofs, and created a conflagration beyond human control."

At the close of the conversation General Sherman intimated that the gentlemen had better retire to rest ; that he would have them called at any hour that the train might be in readiness ; and that, at all events, they should be ready to proceed by sunrise. Governor Graham was invited to occupy the General's tent, and they shared the same apartment. Every courtesy was extended to the other members of the commission.

And now occurred one of those little coïncidences which brighten life under its best aspects, and which are capable of giving pleasure even in such dispiriting circumstances as these ; which, from constitutional predilections, no man appreciates more highly than

Governor Swain, and which, perhaps, for that very reason, happen more frequently to him than to most men. One of General Sherman's aids approached the Governor, inviting him to go with him—that he had vacated his tent for his benefit. The Governor replied that he must object to turning him out, but would occupy it with him with pleasure. The officer replied that he could find a lodging elsewhere, and wished to make the Governor comfortable. He then apologized for desiring to introduce himself, by remarking that no name was more familiar than Governor Swain's in his mother's household. The Governor inquired his name, and found him to be the son of a school-companion, the beloved friend of earlier years, a lady of rare merits and accomplishments, who had long since entered upon her rest. She, with the mother of Governor Vance, had been in early girlhood the Governor's schoolmates, and competitors with him for school distinctions in the most anxious and generous strife he has ever known. Governor Graham and Governor Swain both voted, in 1860, for the uncle of this gallant young officer, for President of the United States, as the advocate of "the Union, the Constitution, and the enforcement of the laws," in the vain hope that the evils which then threatened and have since overwhelmed the country might be averted. To such offered kindness from such a quarter, under such circumstances, one might well respond,

> "I take thy courtesy, by Heaven,
> As freely as 'tis nobly given."

At sunrise the next morning the commissioners proceeded on their return in the train, somewhat in advance of the army, with the understanding that they were to go to Raleigh, notify Governor Vance of the conditions agreed upon, and return to advise General Sherman of their acceptance before he should reach the boundaries of the city.   When within a mile of the capital they saw the flames rising to a great height above the station-house, which had been first plundered and then set on fire by stragglers from the retreating forces of General Wheeler.   The fire put a sudden stop to the progress of the train.   The commissioners alighted, and passed around the blazing building in the hope of finding another train on the other side in which they might proceed to Hillsboro, on the conclusion of their business in Raleigh, but were disappointed.   They went to the house of a friend at the head of Hillsboro street, but found it shut up, and the proprietor a refugee.   They walked the entire length of the street, and did not see a human being till they reached the State House.   Every door was shut, every window-blind was closed.   The same absence of all signs of life, the same death-like silence and air of desertion, the same precautions against intrusion characterized Fayetteville street from the Capitol to the Palace.   The very air seemed shriveled.   In the brief interval that elapsed from the retreat of her protectors to the arrival of her foes, the beautiful city of Raleigh stood under the outstretched arms of her noble oaks, embowered in the luxuriant shrubbery of a thousand gardens, just touched with vernal bloom and radiance—stood with folded hands and drooping head, in all the mortal anguish of suspense, in a silence that spoke, awaiting her fate.

Governor Vance, it was soon ascertained, had left the city, together with all the State officers, having heard the night before that the commission had been captured, and detained as prisoners of war. Despairing then of obtaining any terms from General Sherman, and unwilling to surrender himself unconditionally into his hands, in entire uncertainty of what treatment he might expect, Governor Vance had decided to leave for Hillsboro, after making every possible arrangement for the surrender of the city by.the Mayor and Council. He wrote the following letter to General Sherman, to be delivered by the city authorities:

STATE OF NORTH-CAROLINA, }
EXECUTIVE DEPARTMENT, }
RALEIGH, April 12, 1865. }

General W. T. Sherman, Commanding United States Forces:

GENERAL: His Honor, Mayor William B. Harrison, is authorized to surrender to you the city of Raleigh. I have the honor to request the extension of your favor to its defenseless inhabitants generally; and especially to ask your protection for the charitable institutions of the State located here, filled as they are with unfortunate inmates, most of whose natural protectors would be unable to take care of them, in the event of the destruction of the buildings.

The capitol of the State, with its libraries, museum,

and most of the public records, is also left in your power. I can but entertain the hope that they may escape mutilation or destruction, inasmuch as such evidences of learning and taste can advantage neither party in the prosecution of the war, whether destroyed or preserved.

I am, General, very respectfully,
Z. B. VANCE.

The Governor lingered in Raleigh till midnight, hoping to receive some news of the commission, and then, *without a single member of his staff*, accompanied by Captain Bryan and Captain J. J. Guthrie, who volunteered to escort him, he rode out to General Hoke's encampment, not far from Page's, (Carey's,) some eight miles from the city. Generals Hardee, Hampton, Hoke, and Wheeler, with their commands, had passed through Raleigh in the evening.

Leaving Governor Vance's course for future consideration, I return to the group of gentlemen standing in front of the State House shortly after sunrise on the morning of Thursday, thirteenth. The only person they met at the capitol was the servant who waited in the executive office, and who had been intrusted by Governor Vance with the keys. True to the trust reposed in him, he was present at the proper time to deliver the keys as he had been directed—an instance of fidelity and punctuality under trying circumstances that would, doubtless, have been rewarded with his freedom, even had there been no liberating army at hand. The commission received the key from him, and after a hasty consultation, it was agreed that one should open the State House and remain till the arrival of the Federal army, taking such measures as he might deem most expedient; and that the other should make his way, with the best means he could command, to Hillsboro, taking the University in his way, and endeavoring to provide for the safety of friends and neighbors in that quarter.

When walking from the railroad station to the city, the commissioners had passed through the lines of General Wheeler's cavalry, pressing in the direction of Chapel Hill. Half an hour after reaching the State House, a dozen men, the *débris* of our army, were observed at the head of Fayetteville street, breaking open and plundering the stores. Governor Swain, who had remained at the State House, approached them, and stated that he was immediately from General Sherman's headquarters, and had assurance from him that if no resistance was offered to his advance-guard, the town should be protected from plunder and violence, and urged the soldiers to leave at once and join their retreating comrades. They replied, " D—n Sherman and the town too; they cared for neither." Robert G. Lewis, Esq., the first citizen of Raleigh who had yet been seen, came up just then, and joined his entreaties with earnestness. More and more vehement remonstrances were used without effect, till the head of Kilpatrick's column appeared in sight advancing up the street, when they all, with a single exception, sprang to their horses and started off in full gallop. Their leader, a lieutenant whose name and previous history are yet unknown, mounted his horse, and took his station midway between the old New-Berne bank and the book-store, drew his revolver, and waited till Kilpatrick's advance was within a hundred yards, when he discharged it six times in rapid succession in the direction of the officer at the head of the troops. He then wheeled, put spurs to his horse, and galloped up Morgan street, followed by a dozen fleet horsemen in hot pursuit. Turning a corner his horse fell. He re-mounted, and dashed round the corner at Pleasant's store on Hillsboro street. A few yards further on, near the bridge over the railroad, he was overtaken, and was brought back to the Capitol Square, where General Kilpatrick ordered his immediate execution. It is said that he asked for five minutes' time to write to his wife, which was refused. He was hung in the grove just back of Mr. Lovejoy's, and was buried there. He died bravely — a vile marauder, who justly expiated his crimes, or a bold patriot, whose gallantry deserved a more generous sentence, as friend or foe shall tell his story. No Southerner will cast a reproach on that solitary grave, or will stand beside it with other than feelings of deep commiseration. His crime was more the rash act of a passionate and reckless boy, an aimless bravado from one wild and despairing man to a hundred and twenty thousand. What our soldiers did or did not do in those last dark days of confusion and utter demoralization, we record with sad and ten-der allowance. Wrong was done in many instances, and excesses committed ; but we feel that the remem-brance of their high and noble qualities will in the end survive all temporary blots and blurs. And for those who perished in the wrong-doing engendered by desperation and failure and want, their cause has perished with them. *So perish the memory of their faults!*

Governor Graham, accompanied by Colonel Burr, set out for Hillsboro on foot, the road to Chapel Hill being blocked up by Wheeler's retreating squadrons, and resolved to trust to the chances of obtaining horses by the way. Finding themselves, however, involved in a skirmish between Hampton's rear-guard and Kilpatrick's advance, and in somewhat perilous circumstances, they made the best of their way back to Raleigh, where they arrived in the course of the morning.

Governor Swain, meanwhile, had received at the State House the Federal officer charged with the erection of the national flag over the dome of the building. He met him with the remark, "I am just from your Commanding General, and have his promise that this edifice shall not be injured." The officer replied, "I know you, sir, and have orders to attend to your wishes." They took quiet possession, and the Stars and Stripes were soon waving from the summit. Governor Swain remained at the capitol, in company with Mayor Harrison, who, assisted by Mayor Devereux, Major Hogg, and Surgeon-General Warren, and other gentlemen, advised with the Provost-Marshal in relation to the stationing of guards for the protection of the citizens, and other matters, until two o'clock, when, with Governor Graham, he went to General Sherman's quarters in the Government house, and delivered the keys to him.

General Sherman regretted Governor Vance's departure from the city, and desired his return as speedily as possible. He therefore wrote him a letter inviting his return, and inclosing a safe-conduct through his lines for him and any members of the State or city government.

HEADQUARTERS RALEIGH, N. C., ⎱
ARMY IN THE FIELD, April 13, 1865. ⎰

To all Officers and Soldiers of the Union Army:

Grant safe-conduct to the bearer of this to any point twelve miles from Raleigh and back, to include the Governor of North-Carolina and any members of the State or city government, on his way back to the capital of the State.   W. T. SHERMAN.

Major-General Commanding.

This letter the commission undertook to transmit to Governor Vance without loss of time; but no horses were to be had among their friends in the city, nor could any messenger be got willing to undertake the errand. As soon as General Sherman heard this, he directed his adjutant-general to furnish the gentlemen with the means of locomotion, which was promptly done. The next morning (Friday) they left Raleigh for Hillsboro, where it was supposed Governor Vance was; passed rapidly through Kilpatrick's columns, and then through Hampton's; had a short interview with the latter at Strayhorns, where he was to spend the night; reached Hillsboro in the evening, and, entering Governor Graham's parlor, found Governor Vance there, with Colonel Ferebee, quietly awaiting intelligence. Till informed by the commissioners, neither he nor General Hampton had heard of the surrender of General Lee, and even then could hardly be induced to believe it.

General Sherman's letter inviting his return to Raleigh was put in his hands, and he was urged to return thither immediately with the commissioners; but he had also just received a dispatch from President Davis, urging him most earnestly to meet him in Greensboro by the returning train. General Johnston had also gone on to Greensboro, and before returning to Raleigh, Governor Vance desired to see both him and the President — the former to get his permission to pass his lines, and the latter, to learn his future plans and acquaint him with his intention to surrender. This much was due, at least in courtesy, to the falling chieftain, though he was President only in name of a nation that had no longer any existence. Governor Vance was never the man to turn his back upon the setting sun to pursue his own advantage. So he decided to obey President Davis's last requisition before accepting General Sherman's invitation, and left Hillsboro for Greensboro on Saturday morning.

Governor Graham remained at home with his family, and Governor Swain proceeded to Chapel Hill, where he arrived on Saturday morning, and found it occupied by General Wheeler's cavalry, General Hoke's command having passed through, pressing on to Greensboro.

CHAPTER XII.

WHEN the retrograde movement of General Johnston's army was at last fairly understood—the supply-
trains moving slowly along the roads of Orange, and
General Wheeler's cavalry, acting upon the maxim
that all that they left behind them was so much aid
and comfort to the enemy, taking care to leave at least
as few horses and mules as possible—then deluded
people, who had all along hugged themselves in the
belief that their remoteness was their security, began
to shake the dust from their eyes, and open them to
admit a view of the possibility of Sherman's army
reaching even their secluded homes.

The mission of Governors Graham and Swain was
not generally understood, even by their near neighbors. That any available attempt to check the ruin
and devastation that had hitherto accompanied that
army could be made, or was even consistent with
honor and our allegiance to the Confederate Government, very few believed. A distinguished Confeder-

ate general, standing on our sidewalk, as his division
of infantry marched through on Friday, fourteenth,
said, in reference to the commissioners, that they were
a couple of traitors, and ought to be hung.   General
Wheeler's cavalry held the village of Chapel Hill until
mid-day of April sixteenth, Easter Sunday.   Not a
house in the place but was thrown open to show them
kindness and hospitality.   There were rough riders
among these troopers—men who, if plunder was the
object, would have cared little whether it was got from
friend or foe.   How much of this disposition to sub-
sist by plunder was due to the West-Point training of
their General, it would perhaps be inquiring too curiously to consider.   A few such reckless men in a regiment would have been enough to entail an evil name
upon the whole; and at the time of which I now speak
there were more than a few in General Wheeler's command who were utterly demoralized, lawless, and de-
fiant.   Having said this much, because the truth must
be told, I will add that of that famous band by far the
greater part were true and gallant men.   We mingled
freely with them, from General Wheeler himself, who
slept in the drenching rain among his men, and was
idolized by them, to his poorest private, and the impression made by them was altogether in their favor.
There were men from every Southern State, and from
every walk in life.   There were mechanics from Georgia and planters from Alabama: one of the latter I especially remember, who had been a country physician
in the north-east corner of the State; a frank and
steady, gray-haired man, whose very address inspired

confidence, and whose eldest boy rode by his side: there were gay Frenchmen from Louisiana and lawyers from Tennessee, some of whom had graduated at this university in the happy days gone by, who revisited these empty corridors with undisguised sadness, foreboding that not one stone would be left upon another of these venerable buildings, perhaps not an oak left standing of the noble groves, after Sherman's army had passed. Many of these men had not been paid one cent, even of Confederate currency, in more than a year. Few of them had more than the well-worn suit of clothes he had on, the inefficient arms he carried, and the poor and poorly equipped horse he rode. A lieutenant, not four years before a graduate of this university, who had not seen his home within a year, and who had not long before received intelligence that his house in Tennessee had been burned to the ground by the enemy, and that his wife and child were homeless, when the certain news was brought by Governor Swain of General Lee's surrender, covered his face with his hands to hide a brave man's tears. He told us that a twenty-five cent Confederate note was all that he possessed in the world besides his horse. The privates generally discussed the situation of affairs calmly and frankly, and with an amount of intelligence that the Southern and South-western yeomanry have not generally had credit for possessing. They one and all agreed that, if the end was near, they would not surrender. "No, no," said a red-cheeked Georgian boy of nineteen, "they won't get me;" and one six-foot-six saturnine Kentuckian assured me that he would join the army of France, and take his allegiance and his revolver over the water. I trust he is on his little farm, by the Licking River, as I write, and has found him a wife, and is settled down to do his whole duty to the country once more.

These men rode up frankly to our gates. "May I have my dinner here?" "Can you give me a biscuit?" Well, it was not much we had, but we gave it joyfully—dried fruit, sorghum, dried peas, and early vegetables. Poor as it was, we seasoned it with the heartiest good-will and a thousand wishes that it were better. The divisions of infantry passed through at a rapid step without halting, so that we could give them no more than the mute welcome and farewell, and a hearty God bless them, as they passed. Their faces were weather-beaten but cheery; their uniforms were faded, stained, and worn; but they stepped lightly, and had a passing joke for the town gazers, and a kindly glance for the pretty girls who lined the sidewalks, standing in the checkered shade of the young elms.

On Friday afternoon General Wheeler rode in from the Raleigh road with his staff, and alighted at the first corner. One of his aids came up with a map of North-Carolina, which he unrolled and laid on the ground. General Wheeler knelt down to consult it, and the group gathered round him. Several of our citizens drew near, and a circle of as bright eyes and fair faces as the Confederacy could show anywhere, eager to look upon men whose names had been familiar for four years, and whose fame will be part of our national history.

The Federal cavalry were in close pursuit, and several skirmishes had taken place on the road from Raleigh. A brigade under General Atkins followed General Wheeler, while Kilpatrick, with the rest of his division, followed Hampton toward Hillsboro, along the Central Railroad line. The last skirmish occurred, and perhaps the last blood of the war was shed on Friday evening, fourteenth, at the Atkins Plantation, eight miles from Chapel Hill, near the New-Hope River, which was much swollen by heavy rains, and the bridge over which, as well as all others on the road, was destroyed by General Wheeler's men. They attacked the enemy endeavoring to cross on fallen trees and driftwood, and several were killed on both sides. Some of our men were killed in a skirmish at Morrisville, and some of the wounded came on with the trains. One poor fellow from Selma, Ala., mortally wounded, was carried to the house of one of our principal physicians, and tenderly cared for, for two or three days, while he talked of his distant home and his mother, and sent messages to those who would see him no more. After his comrades had passed on and the place was in the hands of the Federals, he resigned himself to die with childlike patience, asking for a favorite hymn, and begging the lovely girl who had watched him with a sister's fidelity to kiss him, as he was dying, " for his sister." He was laid to rest in the garden, and perhaps as bitter tears of regret and despair fell on that lonely grave as on any during the war; for the war was over, and he and the rest had died in vain.

On Sunday, at two P.M., General Wheeler called in his pickets; and once more, and for the last time, we saw the gallant sight of our gray-clad Confederate soldiers, and waved our last farewell to our army. A few hours of absolute and Sabbath stillness and silence ensued. The groves stood thick and solemn, the bright sun shining through the great boles and down the grassy slopes, while a pleasant fragrance was wafted from the purple panicles of the Paullonia. All that nature can do was still done with order and beauty, while men's hearts were failing them for fear, and for looking after those things which were coming on the earth.

We sat in our pleasant piazzas and awaited events with quiet resignation. The silver had all been buried—some of it in springs, some of it under rocks in the streams, some of it in fence-corners, which, after the fences had been burned down, was pretty hard to find again; some of it in the woods, some of it in the cellars. There was not much provision to be carried off—that was one comfort. The sight of our empty store-rooms and smoke-houses would be likely to move our invaders to laughter. Our wardrobes were hardly worth hiding—homespun and jeans hung placidly in their accustomed places. But the libraries, public and private, the buildings of the university—all minor selfish considerations were merged in a generous anxiety for these. So we talked and speculated, while the very peace and profound quiet of the place sustained and soothed our minds. Just at sunset a sedate and soldierly-looking man, at the head of a dozen *dressed in blue*, rode quietly in by the Raleigh road. Governor Swain, accompanied by a few of the principal citizens, met them at the entrance, and stated that he had General Sherman's promise that the town and university should be saved from pillage. The soldier replied that such were his orders, and they should be observed. They then rode in, galloped up and down the streets inquiring for rebels ; and being informed that *there were none* in town, they withdrew for the night to their camp ; and the next morning, being Easter Monday, April seventeenth, General Atkins, at the head of a detachment of four thousand cavalry, entered about eight A.M., and we were captured.

That was surely a day to be remembered by us all. For the first time in four years we saw the old flag— the "Stars and Stripes," in whose defense we would once have been willing to die, but which certainly excited very little enthusiasm now. Never before had we realized how entirely our hearts had been turned away from what was once our whole country, till we felt the bitterness aroused by the sight of that flag shaking out its red and white folds over us. The utmost quiet and good order prevailed. Guards were placed at every house immediately, and with a promptness that was needful ; for one residence, standing a little apart, was entered by a squad of bummers in advance of the guard, and in less than ten minutes the lower rooms, store-rooms, and bed-rooms were overhauled and plundered with a swift and business-like thoroughness only attainable by long and extensive practice. A guard arriving, they left ; but their plunder was not restored. The village guards, belonging to the Ninth Michigan cavalry, deserve especial mention as being a decent set of men, who, while they were here, behaved with civility and propriety.

That was surely a day to be remembered by us all; yet the first returning anniversary of that day brought the village of Chapel Hill an occasion as generally interesting, but invested with a tenderness of its own. On the sixteenth of April, 1866, the whole town poured out to receive two Confederate soldiers—two brothers—who had fallen in battle in our defense.* They came back home that day, and were placed side by side in that church, whose aisles their infant feet had trodden. The plain deal boxes that inclosed them were graced with garlands, and the emblem of the holy faith in which they had died "more than conquerors," woven of the flowers of their own dear native State. It was all that North-Carolina could do for her sons who had died in obedience to her laws.

> Come, Southern flowers, and twine above their grave;
>   Let all our rath spring blossoms bear a part;
> Let lilies of the vale and snowdrops wave,
>   And come thou too, fit emblem, bleeding-heart!
>
> Bring all our evergreens—the laurel and the bay,
>   From the deep forests which around us stand;
> They know them well, for in a happier day
>   They roamed these hills and valleys hand in hand.
>
> Ye winds of heaven, o'er them gently sigh,
>   And April showers fall in kindliest rain,

---

* Junius C. and W. Lewis, the two youngest sons of the Hon. W. H. Battle.

And let the golden sunbeams softly lie
    Upon the sod for which they died in vain.

It was something—it was much, that we could lay
them among their own familiar hills, pleasant in their
lives and undivided in their deaths.   And North-
Carolina dust will lie lightly on their gentle and noble
breasts.

While the command of General Atkins remained in
Chapel Hill—a period of nearly three weeks—the same
work, with perhaps some mitigation, was going on in
the country round us, and around the city of Raleigh,
which had marked the progress of the Federal armies
all through the South.   Planters having large families
of white and black were left without food, forage, cattle, or change of clothing.   Being in camp so long,
bedding became an object with the marauders; and
many wealthy families were stripped of what the industry of years had accumulated in that line.   Much
of what was so wantonly taken was as wantonly destroyed and squandered among the prostitutes and
negroes who haunted the camps.   As to Raleigh,
though within the corporate limits, no plundering of
the houses was allowed; yet in the suburbs and the
country the inscrutable policy of permitting unrestrained license to the troops prevailed to its widest
extent.   From the statements of several of the prominent citizens of Raleigh I make the following extracts,
the first giving a general view, and the other simply
one man's personal experience :

" Immediately around Raleigh the farms were completely despoiled of every thing in the shape of provi-

sions and forage, so as to leave literally nothing for the support of man or beast. In many instances the houses were burned or torn to pieces, and the fences and inclosures entirely destroyed, so as to render it impossible at that season of the year to produce one third of a crop, even with the greatest industry and attention. Every horse and mule found in the country fit for service was taken off, and only a few old and half-starved ones are to be found on the farms."

The other statement I give in full :*

" On the thirteenth day of April, General Sherman took military possession of Raleigh. A portion of his body-guard pitched their tents (eight in number) in my front-yard, which, with a room in my office, were occupied by officers. Their servants—cooks, waiters, and hostlers—took possession of my kitchens, out-houses, and stables, appropriating them in a most riotous and insolent manner. The soldiers tore down my yard and garden-fences for fuel and tents, and turned their horses and mules upon my vegetables and fruit-trees, destroying a large lot of corn, potatoes, peas, etc.; took off my horses and mules, tore off the doors, flooring, and weather-boarding of my out-houses and barns for tents; killed all my poultry, upward of thirty young hogs, cooking them in my kitchen for the officers' tables. After the removal of this squad, another took instant possession, and pitched twenty-four tents in my front-yard and a large number in the lower part

---

* There seems to be no good reason to refrain from saying that this statement describes the treatment received by Governor Manly, and that the lady mentioned in the next paragraph is the wife of General Cox.—EDITOR.

of my grounds, still using my kitchen, beside building
fires all over the yard. At my plantation, three miles
from town, the devastation was thorough and unsparing. I had no overseer there. The negroes, some
seventy in number, were plundered of their clothing
and provisions, consisting of bacon, pickled beef, corn-
meal, and flour. My dwelling-house was broken open,
weather-boarding, flooring, and ceiling carried off,
every window-sash and glass broken out, and every
article of furniture for house or kitchen either carried
off or wantonly destroyed. Barns, cotton-house, and
sheds were all torn down; blacksmith's, carpenter's,
and farming implements carried off or broken up;
three carts and two large wagons, with their gear, destroyed; the fences burned; and a large number of
mules and horses pastured on the wheat-fields; all my
mules and horses there (seventeen in number) carried
off; fifty head of cattle, forty sheep, fifty hogs, and a
large flock of geese and poultry either taken off or
wantonly shot down; a quantity of medicine, some
excellent wines, brandy, whisky, and two hundred
gallons of vinegar were taken. Wagon-trains went
down day after day, till 150 barrels of corn, 15,000
pounds of fodder, 12,000 pounds of hay, and all my
wheat, peas, cotton, etc., were carried off, leaving the
whole place entirely bare, so that my negroes had to
come in town for rations."

By the above account it will be seen that the having a guard did not avail to protect the premises, even
within the city, though, as a general rule, their presence did avail to protect the grounds immediately

around the house. A lady residing beyond the city limits, the wife of a general officer in our army, had her house repeatedly pillaged, and all the provisions belonging to her negroes, as well as her own, carried off. The tent of a general in the Federal army was pitched just in front of the house, and every marauder going in and coming out laden with spoils was immediately in his view; yet not a word was said to check the men, nor any steps allowed for her protection. A guard was refused her, on the ground of the action of Wheeler's men at their entrance; and when, after repeated solicitation, a guard reluctantly came, he allowed all who were on the premises laden, to march off with what they had in hand, saying he had no authority to take any thing away from them! The unfortunate negroes were the severest sufferers, they being literally stripped of their all, and, beginning a new life of freedom, began it without even the little savings and personal property accumulated in slavery.

That General Sherman was well aware of all this, and not only tacitly permitted it, but considered it a necessary part of war that non-combatants lying at the mercy of his army should receive no mercy at all, is one of the extraordinary developments of the war. There would rather seem to be a deficiency of judgment on his part than a real want of humanity, for which he may have been indebted to the astute military training received at West-Point.

To that institution alone must be conceded the unenviable distinction of sending out soldiers instructed to carry fire, famine, and slaughter through the invaded country, and then sententiously declaring that " *such is war*."

> " To her alone the praise is due,
> She let them loose and cried Halloo!"

Even while the peace negotiations were in progress, as we have seen, and in many cases after peace was declared, the grand army hastened to improve the shining hours in Wake, Orange, and Alamance. Wholesale robbery, abuse, and insult were practiced in so many instances under the eyes of the commanding officers, that those who would have said that the *officers* did not know or permit such things, and that they were the work of only lawless stragglers and camp-followers, such as are found in all armies, were forced to the unavoidable conclusion that this species of warfare was encouraged and approved by the commanders as an important branch of the service, and an invaluable aid in the work of subjugation and reconstruction.

CHAPTER XIII.

CORRESPONDENCE BETWEEN GOVERNOR SWAIN AND GENERAL
SHERMAN—GOVERNOR VANCE'S POSITION AND CONDUCT—
KILPATRICK — THE CONDUCT OF THE SERVANTS — "LEE'S
MEN"—PRESIDENT LINCOLN.

I AM persuaded that it requires the exercise of an
implicit faith, and a total rejection of the evidence of
things seen, to believe that General Sherman as a man,
deplored the policy which, as a general, he felt bound
to pursue. I shall, however, give him the benefit of
his own professions, which, whether sincere or not,
are certainly in unison with the part he played in the
treaty with General Johnston. The following correspondence will be read with interest:

CHAPEL HILL, April 19, 1865.

*Major-General W. T. Sherman, commanding United
States Forces:*

GENERAL: . . . On my return to this village
on Saturday morning, fifteenth instant, I found that
General Wheeler, with his division of cavalry, had
been encamped here for two days. He resumed his
march on Sunday morning, leaving the country de-
nuded to a considerable extent of forage, and taking
with him a number of horses and mules. General

Atkins arrived with his brigade on Monday morning, and is in camp here now. I have had several interviews with General Atkins, and have pleasure in stating that he manifests a disposition to execute his orders with as much forbearance as he deems compatible with the proper discharge of his duty. Nevertheless, many worthy families have been stripped by his soldiers of the necessary means of subsistence. A Baptist clergyman—a most estimable, quiet, and charitable citizen, and the most extensive farmer within a circle of three miles—is almost entirely destitute of provision for man and beast; and with a family of more than fifty persons, (white and colored,) has not a single horse or mule. Other instances, not less striking, exist, of families in less affluent circumstances; but I refer particularly to Mr. Purefoy, because he has been my near neighbor for about thirty years, and I hold him in the highest estimation. He, like many others, is not merely without the present means of subsistence, but unless his horses and mules are restored or replaced, can make no provision for the future. The delay of a few days even may render it impossible to plant corn in proper time.

I am satisfied from the impression made on me in our recent interview, that personally, you have no disposition to add to the unavoidable horrors of war, by availing yourself of the utmost license which writers on the subject deem admissible, but that, on the contrary, you would prefer to treat the peaceful tillers of the soil with no unnecessary harshness. I venture to hope, therefore, that the present state of negotiations between the contending armies will enable you to relax the severity of the orders under which General Atkins is acting, and I am satisfied that if you shall feel yourself justified by the course of events in doing so, an intimation of your purpose will be welcome intelligence to him.

I am, very respectfully, your obedient servant,

D. L. SWAIN.

HEADQUARTERS MILITARY DIVISION OF THE
MISSISSIPPI, IN THE FIELD,
RALEIGH, N. C., April 22, 1865.

Hon. D. L. Swain, Chapel Hill, N. C.:

MY DEAR SIR: Yours of April nineteenth was laid before me yesterday, and I am pleased that you recognize in General Atkins a fair representative of our army.

The moment war ceases, and I think that time is at hand, all seizures of horses and private property will cease on our part. And it may be that we will be able to spare some animals for the use of the farmers of your neighborhood. There now exists a species of truce, but we must stand prepared for action; but I believe that in a very few days a definitive and general peace will be arranged, when I will make orders that will be in accordance with the new state of affairs.

I do believe that I fairly represent the feelings of my countrymen—that we prefer peace to war; but if war is forced upon us, we must meet it; but if peace be possible, we will accept it, and be the friends of the farmers and working classes of North-Carolina, as well as actual patrons of churches, colleges, asylums, and all institutions of learning and charity. Accept the assurances of my respect and high esteem.

I am, truly yours,   W. T. SHERMAN,
                           Major-General Commanding.

Without ascribing to General Sherman any extraordinary degree of merit as a writer, I am inclined to give him credit for sincerity in these professions, simply because of the corroborating evidence afforded by his conduct in the treaty with Johnston. Their first agreement was not ratified at Washington, and General Sherman's position therein was severely censured; but no one who rightly estimated the condition of the South at the close of the war, and the state of public feeling among us, has ever doubted that, if that treaty had been ratified, the happiest results would have followed, and an immense amount of trouble, expense, and evil would have been avoided by the whole country. I repeat what I have said previously, that General Sherman alone, of all the prominent men and leaders among our antagonists, was at that time possessed of the requisite ability and statesmanship and magnanimity to comprehend the situation, and seize the opportunity and the means for an equitable adjustment of our difficulties. I greatly regret not being able to present my readers with a copy of his letter of invitation to Governor Vance to return to Raleigh. On the fourteenth of April General Johnston sent him his first letter, requesting a suspension of hostilities, with a view to entering into arrangements for putting a stop to the war. This application was replied to by General Sherman in a really noble and generous spirit, and their correspondence resulted in those interviews at Durham's Station, on the North-Carolina Central Railroad, which concluded the war and have become historical. No one can read that correspondence without seeing unmistakable evidence that General Sherman manifested an eager anxiety to save the South from further devastation. Perhaps a late remorse had touched him; but however that may be, in the *civil* policy he has always advocated toward the South, he has shown himself at once generous and politic. If he had pursued an equally far-sighted course as a soldier; if he had advocated a humane forbearance toward the defenseless people who were crushed beneath his march; if he had enforced a strict discipline in his army, and chosen to appear as a restorer rather than as a destroyer, there are few at the South who would not join to pronounce him the hero of the war on the Northern side, and his name would worthily go down to posterity by the side of the great captain of the age, who declared, when leading his victorious veterans into France, that rather than suffer them to pillage the country as they passed, he would resign his command.

.   .   .   .

While Generals Johnston and Sherman were engaged in their negotiations at Durham's, Governor Vance found that by having obeyed President Davis's summons to Greensboro before accepting General Sherman's invitation to Raleigh, he was effectually pre-

cluded from all further participation in the affairs of
the State. I am not at liberty to say why or how this
was; but it is probable the Governor himself does not
very deeply regret it, since it is not likely he would
have been permitted by the Federal authorities to retain his office, even if he had returned to Raleigh and
resumed the reins. All General Sherman's views and
official acts as peacemaker were speedily disavowed
and overruled at Washington; and though Governor
Vance was willing to have made the experiment, being urged thereto by his best friends, yet, as *matters
have since turned out*, it is as well that he was prevented. He and his noble State were equally incapa-
ble of any attempt to make terms for themselves, even
had it been likely that any terms would have been
granted. Our fortunes were to be those of our sister
States whom we had joined deliberately, fought for,
and suffered with; and Governor Vance was never
more truly our representative than in the treatment
he received from the Federal Government after the
surrender.

Our Governor left Hillsboro on Saturday, arrived in
Greensboro on Sunday morning, April sixteenth, and
found that President Davis had left for Charlotte the
day before. The whole Confederate Government left
Danville the preceding Monday, April tenth, arrived
at Greensboro on the same day, and had ever since
been living in the cars around the railroad station at
that place. Mr. Trenholm being very ill, had been
taken to Governor Morehead's. But the Confederate
President, and all the Government officials lived for

five rainy days in the miserable leaky cars that had brought them thither, having abundant government stores of provision in their train.   On the slope of a hill near by, which tradition points out as that on which General Greene had held a council of war previous to the battle of Guilford, in 1781, President Davis and his Cabinet, and Generals Beauregard and Johnston held their last conference a day or two before Governor Vance's arrival.   It had resulted in the first terms which General Johnston was authorized to make with General Sherman, and he was already on his way back to Hillsboro, to hold his first interview with the Federal commander.   Failing to see the President, Governor Vance would now have returned to Raleigh.   All that can be said at this point is, that he *was not permitted by our military authorities to pass hrough their lines while the negotiations were pending.* He then followed President Davis to Charlotte, and had a final interview with him, giving him notice of his intention, as General Johnston was then on the point of surrendering the army, to surrender himself to Sherman, and use what means were in his power to save the State and State property from further ruin, treating the Confederacy as at an end.   Returning to Greensboro, he found the first terms agreed upon had been rejected at Washington, and the two commanding generals were engaged in a fresh negotiation. Failing still to receive permission to proceed to Raleigh, he wrote a letter to General Sherman, and sent it by Treasurer Worth, who found on his arrival in Raleigh that General Sherman was gone, and General

Schofield was in command, who refused to allow Governor Vance to return at all.

The Governor then remained quietly in Greensboro until Schofield's arrival there, when he had an interview with him, giving him necessary information as to State property, records, etc., etc., and bespeaking his protection for them and for our people, especially in those localities where they were at feud with each other. He then tendered his own surrender, which General Schofield refused to accept, saying he had no orders to arrest him, and he might go where he pleased. Governor Vance then told him he would join his family at Statesville, and would be found there if requisition should be made for him. He arrived in Statesville, rejoining his family on the fourth of May—by a curious coïncidence, the very day on which, four years before, he had left them, a volunteer for the war! And four such years!—sketched for us thirty years ago in that sublime and solemn picture upon the canvas of Webster, where lay a land rent with civil feuds, and drenched in fraternal blood. He remained until the thirteenth, when he was arrested by order of the Federal Government, by Major Porter, commanding a detachment of three hundred cavalry, Ninth Pennsylvania, conveyed a prisoner to Raleigh, and thence to the Old Capitol Prison at Washington City.

On the thirteenth of April, General Sherman entered Raleigh. The day before, General Stoneman had occupied Salisbury. He entered the State from Knoxville, Tenn., taking most of the towns in his way, and committing an immense amount of damage, and

finally arriving in Salisbury just in time to destroy
utterly all the valuable State and Confederate property which had been so sedulously conveyed from Raleigh, to escape General Sherman! The particulars
of this important and successful move I have as yet
been unable to procure. I hope, however, to present
them at some time in a detailed and authentic narrative. The coöperation with Sherman was timely, and
would have been a perfect success if Stoneman had
ventured to hold Salisbury. He might easily have
done so, though, to be sure, he did not know that;
but if he had, he might have given checkmate to the
Confederacy at once. President Davis would never
have reached Charlotte. As it was, the raiders from
Stoneman's command, who cut the Danville road
above Greensboro, were within half an hour of capturing the whole Confederate Government in its flight.

During the occupation of Chapel Hill by Kilpatrick's cavalry, the citizens of the place possessed their
souls in as much patience as they could muster up, endeavoring to arrive at a stoical not to say philosophi-
cal frame of mind, in view of the sudden dislocation
of all things — among other things, maintaining a decent degree of composure upon the establishment of
Liberia in our midst, and accommodating ourselves to
this new phase of things with a good deal of grim
humor. The negroes, however, behaved much better,
on the whole, than Northern letter-writers represent
them to have done. Indeed, I do not know a race
more studiously misrepresented than they have been
and are at this present time. They behaved well

during the war: if they had not, it could not have
lasted eighteen months. They showed a fidelity and
a steadiness which speaks not only well for themselves
but well for their training and the system under which
they lived. And when their liberators arrived, there
was no indecent excitement on receiving the gift of
liberty, nor displays of impertinence to their masters.
In one or two instances they gave "Missus" to understand that they desired present payment for their
services in gold and silver, but, in general, the tide of
domestic life flowed on externally as smoothly as ever.
In fact, though of course few at the North will believe
me, I am sure that they felt for their masters, and
secretly sympathized with their ruin. They knew
that they were absolutely penniless and conquered;
and though they were glad to be free, yet they did
not turn round, as New-England letter-writers have
represented, to exult over their owners, nor exhibit
the least trace of New-England malignity. So the
bread was baked in those latter days, the clothes were
washed and ironed, and the baby was nursed as zealously as ever, though both parties understood at once
that the service was voluntary. The Federal soldiers
sat a good deal in the kitchens; but the division being
chiefly composed of North-western men, who had little
love for the negro, (indeed I heard some d—n him as
the cause of the the war, and say that they would
much rather put a bullet through an abolitionist than
through a Confederate soldier,) there was probably
very little incendiary talk and instructions going on.
In all which, in comparison with other localities, we
were much favored.

So we endeavored to play out the play with dignity and self-possession, watching the long train of foragers coming in every day by every high-road and by-way leading from the country, laden with the substance of our friends and neighbors for many miles, (though in many cases, let me say, the Government made payment for food and forage taken after peace was declared,) watching them with such feelings as made us half ashamed of our own immunity, wondering where it would all end, and that we should have lived to see such a day; reviewing the height from which we had fallen, and struggling, I say, to wear a look of proud composure, when all our assumed stoicism and resignation was put to flight by the appearance, on a certain day, of a squad of unarmed men in gray, dusty and haggard, walking slowly along the road. A moment's look, a hasty inquiry, and "*Lee's men!*" burst from our lips, and tears from our eyes. There they were, the heroes of the army of Virginia, walking home, each with *his pass* in his pocket, and nothing else. To run after them, to call them in, to feel honored at shaking those rough hands, to spread the table for them, to cry over them, and say again and again, "God bless you all; we are just as proud of you, and thank you just as much as if it had turned out differently;" this was a work which stirred our inmost souls, and has left a tender memory which will outlast life. Day after day we saw them, sometimes in twos and threes, sometimes in little companies, making the best of their way toward their distant homes, penniless and dependent on wayside charity for their food, plodding along, while the blue jackets pranced gayly past on the best blood of Southern stables. But I am glad to record that wherever a Federal soldier met any of them, he was prompt to offer help and food, and express a kindly and soldierly cordiality. Grant's men, they all said, had been especially generous. There was something worth studying in the air and expression of these men, a something which had a beneficial and soothing effect on the observers. They were not unduly cast down, nor had any appearance of the humiliation that was burning into our souls. They were serious, calm, and self-possessed. They said they were satisfied that all had been done that could be done, and they seemed to be sustained by the sense of duty done and well done, and the event left to God, and with His award they had no intention of quarreling. It was a fair fight, they said, but the South had been starved out; one dark-eyed young South-Carolinian said, for his part he was going home to settle down, and if any body ever said "secesh" to him again, he meant to knock 'em over. Many looked thin and feeble; and a gallant major from Fayetteville told me himself that when ordered to the last charge, he and his men, who had been living for some days on parched corn, were so weak that they reeled in their saddles. "But we would have gone again," he added, "if Lee had said so."

The news of the death of President Lincoln, received at first with utter incredulity, deepened the gloom and horrible uncertainty in which we lived.

That he was dead simply may not have excited any regret among people who for four years had been learning to regard him as the prime agent in all our troubles. But when the time, place, and manner of his death came to be told, an unaffected and deep horror and dismay filled our minds. The time has not yet come for Southern people to estimate President Lincoln fairly. We never could admire him as he appeared as a candidate for the Presidency, nor look upon him as a great man, in any sense of the word. But even if we had recognized him as a lofty and commanding genius, fit to guide the destiny of a great nation through a crisis of imminent peril, the smoke of the battle-fields would have obscured to us all his good qualities, and we should have regarded him only as the malignant star, whose ascendency boded nothing but evil to us. He was always presented to us in caricature. The Southern press never mentioned him but with some added *sobriquet* of contempt and hatred. His simplicity of character and kindliness of heart we knew nothing of; nor would many now at the South, much as they may deplore his death, concede to him the possession of any such virtues. They judged him by the party which took possession of him after his inauguration, and by his advisers. But a sense of remorse fills my mind now as I write of him, realizing how much that was really good and guileless, and well-intentioned and generous, may have come to an untimely end in the atrocious tragedy at Ford's Theatre. The extravagance of eulogy by which the Northern people have sought to express their sense of his worth and of his loss, has had much to do with our unwillingness to judge him fairly.   To place the Illinois lawyer by the side of Washington would have been an offense against taste and common-sense; but to compare him to the SON OF GOD, to ascribe to him also the work of " dying the just for the unjust," is an impious indecency which may suit the latitude of Mr. Bancroft, and the overstrained tone of the Northern mind generally, but whose only effect at the South is to widen the distance between us and the day when we shall frankly endeavor to understand and do justice to President Lincoln.

CHAPTER XIV.

GENERAL STONEMAN—OUTRAGES—COLD-BLOODED MURDERS—
GENERAL GILLAM — PROGRESS THROUGH LENOIR, WILKES,
SURRY, AND STOKES—STONEMAN'S DETOUR INTO VIRGINIA—
THE DEFENSE OF SALISBURY—THE FIGHT IN THE STREETS OF
SALISBURY — GENERAL POLK'S FAMILY — TEMPORARY OCCU-
PANCY OF SALISBURY—CONTINUOUS RAIDING.

On the same day that General Sherman entered
Raleigh, General Stoneman occupied Salisbury, April
12–13th, thus completing the chain of events which
was closing in upon the Confederacy. Among the
prisoners kept at Salisbury were some of the better
class, who were at large on *parole*. This they broke
in the winter of 1864–'5, and, making their escape over
the mountains into Tennessee, carried such accounts
of the accumulation of stores, etc., at Salisbury, as
made its capture an object of importance.

General Stoneman entered the State during the last
week of March, by the turnpike leading from Taylorsville, Tennessee, through Watauga county to Deep
Gap, on the Blue Ridge. His force was probably six
or seven thousand strong, though rumor increased it
to fifteen, twenty, thirty, and in one instance to sixty
thousand.

They entered Boone, the county-seat of Watauga,

on the twenty-sixth of March.   The village was completely taken by surprise.   No one was aware of the
approach of an enemy till the advance-guard dashed
up the main street, making no demand for surrender,
but firing right and left at every moving thing they
saw.   Mrs. James Council, hearing the noise, stepped
into her piazza with her child in her arms, and immediately a volley of balls splintered the wood-work all
around her.   She, however, escaped unhurt.   The people of this county had been warmly attached to the
Confederate cause, and had bravely resisted East-Tennessee raiders and marauders.   The county-seat was
therefore, perhaps, especially obnoxious; and whatever may have been General Stoneman's policy, there
were subordinate officers in his command who were
only too happy in the opportunity to retort upon a
defenseless and unresisting population.   The jail was
burned by order of General Gillam.   For this it is said
he was sternly rebuked by General Stoneman ; but all
the county records, books, and private papers were
destroyed.   Private houses were of course plundered,
and the citizens were consoled by the assurance that
" Kirk was to follow and clean them out."   Several
citizens were shot under circumstances of peculiar ag-
gravation.   A party of the raiders went into the field
of Mr. Jacob Council, where he was plowing with a
negro.   He was over the conscript age, a prudent,
quiet man, who had taken no part in the war.   He
was shot down in cold blood, notwithstanding his piteous appeals for mercy, because, upon the negro's
statement, he was " an infernal rebel."   Another, War-

ren Green, was killed while holding up his hands in token of surrender.   Another, Calvin Green, was pursued and surrendered, but they continued firing upon him after his surrender.   He then resolved to defend himself, and fought, loading and firing till he was shot down and left for dead.   He shattered the arm of one of the Federal soldiers, so that it had to be amputated that night.   But instead of dying himself, he recovered, and is now living.   Steele Frazier, a lad of fifteen, was chased by a squad of half a dozen.   He made a running fight of it.   Getting over a fence, he coolly waited till they were within range, and then fired and shot one through.   He then ran again, loading, and turned again and killed another of his pursuers ; and notwithstanding the pursuit was kept up some distance, the balls whistling round him, he finally made good his escape, and will probably make none the worse citizen, when he is grown, for his adventurous boyhood.

Through the whole of this raid General Stoneman is represented to have been apparently anxious to mitigate the distresses and horrors of war as far as was practicable, by courteous and humane treatment of the people.   His record and that of General Palmer are in refreshing contrast to those of his subordinate, General Gillam, and of certain other higher names in the Federal army.   There is one story, however, told of him in Boone, which, after all, may be due to his quartermaster or commissary-in-chief.   Mrs. Council had been kind to some Federal prisoners confined in the jail ; and the invaders hearing of it, requited her by affording her protection during their stay.   Kirk's raiders, however, came down after Stoneman had passed on, and stripped the place of all that had been left — the gallant Colonel Kirk himself making his headquarters with this lady—keeping her a close prisoner in her own room, while he and his men made free with the rest of the house and the premises. That they left little or nothing but the bare walls, may be inferred from General Stoneman's remark on his return to the place after the capture of Salisbury. Standing in the piazza and taking a survey of what had once been a happy and beautiful home — the fencing all gone, the gardens, shrubbery, and yard trampled bare, covered with raw hides of cattle and sheep, decaying carcasses, and all manner of filth—he turned to the lady and said, " Well, Mrs. C., I suppose you hardly know whether you are at home or not."   Gratefully remembering his former courtesy to her, she exerted herself to entertain him with such scanty stores as the raiders had left.   A firkin of uncommonly fine butter had been overlooked by them, and she placed some of this on the table.   The General commended this butter especially, and asked her if she had any more of it.   She told him it was about the only thing to eat she had left, and congratulated herself on its safety under his protection.   What was her mortification, a short time after, to see the firkin ordered out and placed in the General's own provision-wagon.   So much that is favorable to General Stoneman's character has reached me, that I can not help hoping he was ignorant of this unspeakably small transaction.

On the twenty-seventh of March, the column was divided. General Stoneman, with one division, went direct to Wilkesboro. The other, under General Gillam, crossed the Blue Ridge at Blowing Rock, and went to Patterson, in Caldwell county, thence rejoining Stoneman at Wilkesboro. At Patterson General Gillam took the responsibility of ordering the extensive cotton factory there to be burned. General Stoneman is said to have regretted this destruction especially, as Mr. Patterson, the owner, had received a promise that it should be spared, and the people of East-Tennessee had been largely supplied from it. But General Gillam, when not immediately under General Stoneman's eye, could not restrain his propensities. He announced that "the Government had been too lenient, and rebels must look out for consequences," and ordered the torch to be applied.

While the raiders were in the Yadkin river-bottom, they were detained three days by freshets. Small parties scoured the country, carrying off all the horses and mules, and burning the factories. There seemed to be no systematic plan of destruction; for while some mills and factories were burned, others in the same neighborhood and quite as easily accessible were spared. Much depended on the personal character and disposition of the commanding officer of these detachments. If he happened to be a gentleman, the people were spared as much as possible; if he were simply a brute dressed in a little brief authority, every needless injury was inflicted, accompanied with true underbred insolence and malice. The privates always followed the lead of their commander. The factories on Hunting Creek, in the upper part of Tredell, were burned with large quantities of cotton. Eagle Mills alone lost eight hundred bales. Among General Gillam's exploits in Wilkesboro, was the finding the horse of the late General James Gordon in the stable of a brother-in-law of the General. This, General G. immediately, with great intrepidity, " captured ;" and further to impress the family with a sense of his heroic achievement, he had a man to mount the animal and parade him slowly up and down before the door of the house for an hour or two.

Leaving Wilkesboro on the thirty-first of March, General Stoneman moved over into Surry county, in the direction of Mount Airy, and thence into Virginia, aiming for Christiansburg, on the Tennessee Railroad. A portion of the command being detached to Wytheville, was met near that place by General Duke's cavalry, and repulsed, but rallying, took the town and destroyed the depot of supplies there. Having effectually destroyed the road above Wythesville, between New River and Big Lick, General Stoneman turned back upon North-Carolina, reëntering it from Patrick county, Virginia, and marching rapidly through Stokes county, appeared suddenly in Salem and Winston on the tenth of April. Here he sent out various detachments· to cut the North-Carolina Central Road and the Danville and Greensboro Road, destroy bridges, supplies, etc., etc. One of these parties, as I have said before, narrowly missed capturing the train conveying the whole Confederate government, in its flight to Greensboro. They burned the bridge at Jamestown, and were about to fire the depot, but upon a sudden false alarm, fled precipitately withou finishing their work. At High Point they burned the depot and large quantities of government stores, also seventeen hundred bales of cotton belonging to Francis Fries, of Salem. The public buildings and stores at Lexington and Thomasville were saved by the arrival of a body of Ferguson's cavalry, who chased the raiders·back to Salem. The general plan of the whole raid seemed to contemplate the destruction of stores and the cutting off communications without risking a battle.

At Salem and Winston private property was protected, no pillage being permitted. This was probably owing to the fact that the inhabitants having had notice of the approach of the raiders, sent a deputation to meet them and make a formal surrender of the town. I am not aware that a demand for surrender was made of any place during the entire raid, or that any place beside Salem and Winston, which may be regarded as one, offered a surrender. The first notice of the presence of any enemy, in most cases, was given by the unlooked-for arrival of the advance-guard galloping in and taking possession.

At Mocksville, a number of the citizens, supposing it was only a small squad that was hurrying through the country and plundering, prepared to give them a warm reception, and a short distance from town fired upon the advancing column. Soon finding their mistake, they retreated. Threats of burning the village for this audacious thought of resistance were made, but as General Stoneman was pressing forward with all speed upon Salisbury, no time was allowed for any such exchange of compliments.

General Stoneman's *detour* into Virginia had completely mystified the people of North-Carolina. They breathed freely as he passed over the border, and congratulated themselves that the dreaded raid, which for weeks had been anticipated, was so soon at an end. The troops which had been posted by General Beauregard at Salisbury, for its protection, were moved off to Greensboro and to the railroad bridge across the Yadkin, and the town was left with little or no defense. If Stoneman had marched thither from Wilkesboro, he would probably have been repulsed with disaster; for a large body of infantry, with artillery and cavalry, had been concentrated there; but when Salisbury was attacked, on the morning of the twelfth of April, the whole effective force did not much exceed five hundred men, including two batteries on their way to join Johnston at Raleigh. Of these five hundred two hundred were "galvanized" Irish, recruited from among the Federal prisoners—besides artisans in the government employ from the various shops, Junior reserves, and a number of citizens who volunteered in defense of their homes. In the absence of General Bradley T. Johnson, the commandant of the post, General Gardner took command, and disposed his handful of men at various points on the road toward Mocksville, so as to man and support the batteries, there being nowhere more than one hundred and fifty men at any point.

The attack began at daylight.   By eight o'clock the batteries were flanked.   The artillery-men fought bravely, but were of course soon overpowered and compelled to leave their guns in the hands of the enemy.   A few of the "galvanized" Irish fought well, but the majority went over in a body to the Federals soon after the fight commenced, leaving the artillery without support, and of course betraying the weakness of the Confederates.   A desultory fight was kept up till the suburbs of the town were reached, and then all order and subordination were lost, the Confederates scattering through the town and to the woods beyond.   Several of them were wounded, and one or two were killed in the town.   The loss of the Federals is unknown, but several were buried on the battle-field.   A number of Confederates were taken prisoners, some citizens, negroes, etc.   By nine o'clock the place was in quiet possession of the enemy, who galloped in with drawn swords and full of strange oaths.   Many of the citizens, negroes, and children, were in the doors and on the side-walks gazing for the first time at the Federal uniform.   In the desultory running fight that was kept up through the streets, one of the Irish recruits before mentioned, fighting bravely, was shot through the lungs ; but he continued to load and fire as he retreated till he fell on the piazza of Mrs. M. E. Ramsay.   Though the balls fell thick about him, and she was alone with her little children, she went out to him and managed to get him inside the house, where she nursed and stimulated him the greater part of the day, till she could get a physician to him and have him removed to the hospital. He said to her, "They have killed me, but I die a brave man; I fought them as long as I could stand." She supposed that of course his wound was mortal, but a fortnight after, to her astonishment, he returned to thank her for her kindness.

Captain Frank Y. McNeely was found in the Arsenal and shot. Lieutenant Stokes, of Maryland, was sitting on his horse in front of General Bradley Johnson's headquarters, when a squad of the enemy dashed into the street. An officer in front cried out, "There's a d—d rebel—charge him." The Lieutenant waited till the officer was in point-blank range, and then shot him through, and putting spurs to his horse fled—hotly pursued. One of the pursuers was gaining on him, considerably in advance of the rest, and probably intended to sabre him; but the Lieutenant suddenly reining his horse aside, let the raider pass, and as he passed fired and killed him, and then made good his escape. The officer shot proved to be one of General Stoneman's staff.

A small squad of the Confederates retreated fighting through the yard and premises of Frank Shober, Esq. One of their number was killed in the piazza of the house.

This hand-to-hand fighting in the streets—such incidents as these, and the fact that Salisbury was an especial object of hatred to the invaders as the prison depot of so many of their unfortunate comrades, whose graves were to be counted there by thousands—these things certainly gave General Stoneman every excuse for the plunder and destruction of the whole town had he chosen to interpret the laws of war as did General Sherman. But he did not so interpret them; he did not even fall back upon the reserve that he was unable to restrain his justly infuriated soldiers. He declined to avail himself of General Gillam's burning zeal for the honor of the Union. This latter officer was heard to say that, if he had his way, he would make the people of Salisbury think " all hell was let loose upon them." Another account states that he declared that " *though born in Salisbury*, he would be glad to lay it in ashes."*

But General Stoneman's policy toward the inhabitants of Salisbury is a very striking illustration of the principles which, in a previous chapter, I have endeavored to show were the only true and generous and really politic guide for the commanders of an invading army. Private property was protected, guards were stationed, and General Stoneman repeatedly gave strict orders for the enforcement of quiet and protection of the citizens. He himself in person inspected the public stores, which were of course by the laws of war doomed to destruction, and refused to allow the Confederate Quartermaster's depot to be burned lest it should endanger the town. The officers, whether willingly or not, seconded their commander. Whatever plundering and insolence the people were subjected to—and there were a number of such cases

---

* *Is* General Gillam a son of North-Carolina? I put the note and query for the future historian. If so, then we have only another proof that decency and good principles are not always hereditary.

—was very evidently the work of unauthorized bummers, who appeared in mortal dread of the guards, and did their work hurriedly and furtively. Corncribs and smoke-houses were entered, horses and mules and arms were seized; but, on the whole, the general policy was the sound one of protection to noncombatants.

Early in the morning of the attack several large trains with government stores made their escape from Salisbury toward Charlotte and Greensboro, but a passenger train on the Western road was not so fortunate. Having proceeded a mile or two from town, the track was found obstructed; and as soon as the train stopped, a volley was poured into it without any demand for surrender. Several passengers were wounded, but happily none of the ladies, among whom were the widow and daughters of General Leonidas Polk. The cars being set on fire, much of the baggage belonging to the passengers was burned —all that was rescued was plundered—and among Mrs. Polk's valuables were found the sword, uniform, papers, and other cherished relics of her husband. These things were all seized with great triumph, and though much that was taken besides was afterward restored to Mrs. Polk, no inducements could prevail upon the gallant Colonel Slater of the Eleventh Kentucky Cavalry to return to the widowed lady these mementos of her husband. He claimed them as " taken on the battle-field," and kept them.

As soon as the town was quiet, a strong force was detailed to attack the railroad bridge across the

Yadkin, six miles distant. Here strong fortifications on the Davidson side of the river had been erected, under Beauregard's supervision, on a hill commanding the bridge and the Rowan shore. General York of Louisiana, with ten or twelve hundred men—home-guards and "galvanized" Irish—defended the bridge : its preservation was of the greatest importance to the Confederate cause, and strict orders had been issued by General Beauregard to defend it at all hazards. At two o'clock P.M., on the twelfth, the raiders ar-rived, and brisk skirmishing was kept up on the Row-an side. At three o'clock some of the cannon captured in the morning on the other side of Salisbury, were brought down, and opened on the Confederate batter-ies. Heavy cannonading between the two continued till dark, when the raiders, thinking the place too well fortified to risk an assault, returned to Salisbury, de-stroying the railroad as they went. A few Confeder-ates were wounded, one or two were killed. The Federal loss, if any, is unknown.

The assailants returned to assist in the destruction of the public stores at Salisbury, which I have before stated were immense. They had been accumulating there for weeks from Columbia, Charlotte, Richmond, Danville, and Raleigh. The clothing, provisions, med-ical stores, etc., were collected in the main street and fired. The length of four entire squares was occupied by the burning mass, valued at at least a million in specie. Much was given away to negroes and the lower class of the white population—much was quietly appropriated, and by some who should have known better. The distresses and privations of war make times of strong temptation, and the general demoralization that prevailed all over our country was no greater at Salisbury than elsewhere. To people who had been half starved for months, and many of them half clothed, it was hard to see such quantities of sugar, coffee, spice, flour, bacon, luxuries to which they had long been strangers, burning in their streets like so much rubbish. The stores were all emptied besides of private property—and many people were to be seen passing along the streets loaded with what they chose. Many soldiers had dozens of coats, shirts, etc., piled up before them on their horses.

The value of the medical stores alone was estimated at $100,000 in gold. It is a little curious that, while such an amount was being thrown into the flames, one of the surgeons of the Federal army entered the office of one of the principal physicians in the place— Dr. J. J. Summerell—and was about to carry off all his scanty store of medicine; but upon remonstrance, he agreed to *divide*, saying, he could not bear to rob a brother practitioner.

On the night of the 12–13th the ordnance stores, arsenal, foundry, with much valuable machinery, the Government steam distillery, the dépôts and other buildings belonging to both the Central and Western roads, and other public buildings were fired. The night being perfectly still, the sheets of flame rose steadily into the air, and the great conflagration was plainly visible at the distance of fifteen miles; and for several hours the incessant and distinct explosions of

shells and fixed ammunition conveyed the impression
to the anxious watchers, miles away, in the adjoining
counties, that a fierce battle was raging.   There was
no hallooing by the soldiers—no shouts—only the crack-
ling of the flames and the bursting of the shells.   Now
and then a mounted troop swept through the streets,
the horsemen in profound silence, the lurid flames from
the burning distillery making their rough faces look
ghastly enough, while the buttons and other mountings
of their equipments sparkled in the firelight.   No one
thought of sleep that night, not even the children.

A large building, three stories high, originally built
for a cotton factory, but for some time past occupied
by Federal prisoners—all of whom a few weeks previously had been sent to Richmond and Wilmington
for exchange — together with the barracks and all
other buildings connected with it, were burned ; and it
may be well imagined that the Federal soldiers felt a
peculiar satisfaction in the destruction of a spot so
memorable to them—the scene of so much wretched-
ness and want and despair.   Many of the men with
Stoneman had been among the prisoners there, and
many had had brothers and other relatives there.   I
have heard that General Gillam himself had been one
of the number before his promotion.   No one who
knows what the condition of these prisoners was, can
wonder at any amount of rage expressed by the survivors and avengers.   The way in which both sides,
during the war, treated their prisoners, is an exceedingly curious commentary on the boasted Christian
civilization of the whole country, from Maine to Texas.

For the Northern side there is no excuse. For the Southern side there is one—and but one. Our prisoners were starved, as I have said before, because we were starving ourselves; our children were crying for bread, and our soldiers were fighting on half-rations of parched corn and peas. We could not tell our enemies this! We were not to confess to them this fatal weakness in our cause! But what we could do to induce their Government to take these poor wretches home and give us our own in exchange, we did do. Every inducement was offered to them again and again in vain. So far, then, our skirts are clear. But brutality of speech and behavior, cruel indifference to their situation, unnecessary harshness and violence to helpless unarmed men, diseased and dying—of this there may have been much among certain of our officials, and for this we will yet have to repent before Him who hears the sighing of the prisoner.

It has been estimated that the loss in buildings alone, which were mostly of brick, would reach to half a million in specie, and the total loss of all property to several millions. Had the war continued, the capture of Salisbury would have been a stunning blow to General Johnston, and would have severely crippled his movements. As it was, it is a matter of great regret that such a vast amount of most valuable property should have been destroyed just at a time when its destruction was no longer necessary to the overthrow of a cause already dead. General Stoneman might safely have held Salisbury from the hour he entered it, and preserved every dollar's worth of its stores for the advantage of his own government. He might have prevented the further flight of the Confederate Government, and President Davis and all his cabinet might have been forced to surrender with General Johnston. And it would have been better if they had. But General Stoneman did not know what a brilliant part he was playing in the last act of the great tragedy, and he hurried to get through with it and leave Salisbury as rapidly as he had entered it. On the 13th a terrific explosion of the magazine finished the work, and that evening the Federals moved off toward Statesville, riding most of the night as if under apprehension of pursuit.

General Stoneman must certainly be allowed to have accomplished his ends with a skill, celerity, and daring, which entitle him to high praise as a military leader. Add to this the higher praise of humanity, and the ability to control his troops, and he well deserves a higher niche than some who led grand armies on great marches. Salisbury, comparing her lot with that of Columbia and Fayetteville, may well afford to hold General Stoneman's name in grateful remembrance.

I have taken no pleasure in this recital of injuries, insults, inhumanity, and breach of faith. The truth of history demands that the facts shall be told on both sides calmly and with impartiality. The world, which has heard so much of one side, should hear the other too; and posterity, at whose bar we shall all stand for this four years' work, should have every opportunity afforded for a righteous verdict. And there are other

ways in which the truth plainly told may do good.
People will be enabled, looking at these details, to arrive
at a just estimate of what war may become, even
among Christian people, and shudder to invoke its
horrors lightly, and may teach their children so. How
many of us knew in the spring of 1861 what was about
to break out among us—what wide-spread ruin, what
raging passions, what furies of hell, which once evoked
will not down at our bidding? Quiet men, who were
familiar with the pages of European history and knew
what Christian armies had done again and again in
the fairest and most civilized portion of her empires,
these came gravely from their studies with words of
warning to the gay throngs of young people who were
cheering each other on to the impending strife. But
these were the old fogies of that day—cold-blooded—
unpatriotic—who did not love the South. What a
short and brilliant programme was laid down! The
girls made their silken banners, and the boys marched
proudly off to glorious victory; England and France
would see fair play; and this dear and sunny South
was to spring at once upward and onward in a career
of glory. One of the most influential journals in the
South—one of the soberest—dealing lightly and easily
with the great issues of the war; settling at a word
the boundary lines of the new Southern republic, and
dotting what were to be our frontier States with a
chain of forts; establishing the new war office, and the
standing army, henceforth to be a necessary feature,
grew enthusiastic over the splendid resource thus to
be afforded to our " aristocratic young men of family

and fortune." The army was to be especially for the *gentlemen* of the South. Alas! and alas! Now, torn and bleeding and broken-hearted, humiliated, stripped, crushed, disfranchised, and helpless, we may look back and learn a lesson.

It may be well, too, if public attention can be directed by such narratives to an investigation of the laws of war, and some inquiry be suggested as to the necessity of their being revised and mitigated. And it can not but a have a beneficial effect that even victorious military heroes shall be made amenable to public opinion for the manner in which they have wielded the great powers intrusted to them, and find, in some cases, their fresh-plucked laurels withering in their grasp.

The actual loss and injury inflicted by the enemy, in the progress of the war, on personal and public property, was very far from being the greatest evil which its continuance entailed upon us. I speak not now of losses by death. *Inter arma leges silent* is an old saying; and though framed in a dead language, its drift is well understood and acted upon by people who can not even read it. The longer the war lasted the more evident became the demoralization of our people, and their disregard for laws and principles of action by which they had been guided all their lives. At the break-up respectable citizens, who would once have shrunk from even the imputation of such conduct, helped themselves unblushingly to Government stores and public property, even when it had been intrusted to them for safe keeping. When their betters set such an example, the common people of course threw off all restraint; and we could then plainly see how petty, compared with the advantages gained, are the taxes which we pay for the support of law and government. There seemed to be a general feeling, during the last ninety days, that there was no government outside of the military pressure for conscripts, deserters, and tithes. I am reminded of a poor neighbor as I write, who, during the winter of '64–'65, like many others, provided his family with wood to which he had no right. Being remonstrated with, he said with energy, "There is no law in the land in these days," and continued his depredations openly. And I do believe the general feeling was, "What else *can* he do, with wood at forty dollars a cord?"

Nor are such fruits of war confined to the Southern side of the Potomac. The fires that have lit up so many Northern cities; the tales of murder, robbery, and riot, which have crowded the columns of their journals for the past year; and the general lawlessness and contempt of authority which prevail there, point unmistakably to the dangers which accompany a triumphant and utterly undisciplined army, whether in the enemy's land or returning home flushed with victory and demoralized with licensed rapine and riot. Did Northern people soberly believe that it was zeal for the Union and hatred of secession that prompted such wholesale plunder in the South? Let their own experience since, and the records of their criminal courts within the last year, show, that when plunder is to be had, lawless and unrestrained men care little whether it belongs to friend or foe ; and that lust, once aroused and let loose, can not distinguish, and is amenable to no laws.   Herein, as in thousands of other instances, is that saying true, " The measure we mete is measured to us again."

Human nature is indeed a wild beast that has need to be chained and continually surrounded with restraints, or we should prey upon each other as savages do, and so lapse into barbarism.   Let the experience of the last five years teach the people of this great Republic henceforth to preserve indissolubly the bonds of PEACE, that so, as a nation, they may do their appointed part toward hastening on the coming of that PRINCE of whose kingdom there shall be no end.

" Te duce, qui maneant sceleris vestigia nostri
    Irrita perpetuâ solvent formidine terras."*

* With Thee for our guide, whatever relics of our crimes remain shall be taken away, and free the world from perpetual fears.

CHAPTER XV.

STATESVILLE was entered on the night of the 13th, and occupied for a few hours only. Long enough, however, to insure the destruction of the Government stores and railroad dépôt, and of the *Iredell Express* office, a paper which was obnoxious from the warmth with which it had advocated the cause of the Confederacy. No county in the State had suffered more severely than Iredell in the loss of her best and bravest sons in the army. The famous Fourth North-Carolina regiment was composed of Iredell boys, and the colors of no regiment in the service were borne more daringly or more nobly. I remember to have heard it said, after one of the great battles around Richmond, that half the families of Iredell were in mourning. When it became known that the *Express* office was to be burned, the ladies and citizens plead earnestly that it might be spared for the sake

of the town, which was in great danger of being involved in the conflagration. The citizens offered to
tear it down and remove the materials to a vacant
square to be burned, but this was not allowed by the
officer who had charge of the business. The office
was fired where it stood, and in consequence a large
private dwelling, belonging to Dr. Dean, standing near
it, was also consumed, and a large family turned out
houseless and utterly prostrated otherwise—Gen. Sherman's army having just previously destroyed certain
other resources of theirs. The wind providentially
blowing in the right direction, saved the town from
general ruin. One of the citizens, Mr. Frank Bell,
was cruelly beaten and tortured to make him disclose
the hiding-place of gold which they suspected he possessed. He, however, had none.

The raiders moved, on the 14th, to Taylorsville,
Alexander county, and from thence to Lenoir, Caldwell county, which they reached on Saturday, 15th,
and occupied till Monday, 17th. On the road from
Statesville a part of the command was dispatched in
the direction of Lincolntòn, under General Palmer. Of
this officer the same general account is given as of
General Stoneman, that he exhibited a courtesy and forbearance which reflected honor on his uniform, and
have given him a just claim to the respect and grati-
tude of our western people. The following pleasant
story is a sample of his way of carrying on war with
ladies: Mrs. Vance, the wife of the Governor, had
taken refuge, from Raleigh, in Statesville with her
children. On the approach of General Stoneman's army,

she sent off to Lincolnton, for safety, a large trunk filled with valuable clothing, silver, etc., and among other things two thousand dollars in gold, which had been intrusted to her care by one of the banks. This trunk was captured on the road by Palmer's men, who of course rejoiced exceedingly over this finding of spoil, more especially as belonging to the rebel Governor Vance. Its contents were speedily appropriated and scattered. But the circumstance coming to General Palmer's knowledge, within an hour's time he had every article and every cent collected and replaced in the trunk, which he then immediately sent back under guard to Mrs. Vance with his compliments. General Palmer was aiming for Charlotte when he was met by couriers announcing news of the armistice.

There was no plundering allowed in Statesville. Mrs. Vance was treated with respect and entirely unmolested. But several weeks afterward, when Governor Vance was a prisoner in Washington, a squad of Federal soldiers came to her residence and carried away every article of furniture in the house. Some of this belonged to the Mansion House in Raleigh, and had been removed to Statesville for safety at the same time when other Government property was sent off. The officer who was in command had the grace to appear ashamed of his business, and apologized to Mrs. Vance repeatedly, stating that he was acting under orders, and that it was done at the suggestion of North Carolinians in Raleigh, who desired that the articles belonging to the executive mansion should be restored. Every thing in the house was taken away, private property and all, and not one article ever reached the executive mansion. Two queries occur : First, Who were the North-Carolinians who instigated this insult to Mrs. Vance ? And second, Whatever *did* become of the furniture ? Every thing in the way of furniture was carried off, and Mrs. Vance, who was then ill, and her children were left without even a bed. In less than twelve hours after this raid extraordinary became known to the people in the town and neighborhood, the house was entirely refurnished with more than it had contained previously. I can well imagine that there was no one who did not esteem it a privilege thus to testify their love and respect for the Governor and his family.

General Stoneman pressed on toward Tennessee through Watauga county, with the prisoners, leaving General Gillam, with three hundred men, to proceed to Asheville *via* Morganton.

Of the prisoners it was estimated there were about nine hundred. Many of them were old men past the conscript age, some were boys, others were discharged Confederate soldiers in feeble health or maimed, who had been captured at their homes. In regard to them no settled course or plan of action seems to have been adopted. In some instances they easily escaped, or were allowed to do so tacitly, and regained their homes in a short time. Most of them, however, were dragged on with every circumstance of barbarity and cruelty. A few instances may be given illustrative of their treatment.

In Lenoir they were confined in and about the

Episcopal church, under a strong guard, with peremptory orders from General Gillam to shoot every man who attempted to escape. The gallant General added, that he " would rather have ten men shot than one escape." It must be remembered that a number of them were over sixty years of age; some were permanently diseased; some were men who had not walked continuously five miles for years, or perhaps hardly in their whole lives; and that, when they reached Lenoir, they had all of them marched twenty-five and thirty miles in eight or ten hours. They had been double-quicked a good part of the way from Taylorsville to Lenoir, and arrived there on Saturday afternoon nearly exhausted with fatigue and hunger. Notwithstanding their deplorable condition, they had nothing to eat after that march till Sunday at ten A.M., and then they were only partially supplied from the scanty stores of the plundered villagers; for Lenoir, having been pronounced a " rebellious little hole," was sentenced to receive its full share of punishment at the hands of General Gillam. It was not till the afternoon of Sunday that rations were issued. Whenever any of the townspeople carried any thing to the prison, the scene was said to have been most piteous, so many men begging for just one morsel of dry bread. There seemed to be an especial spirit of bitterness toward the prisoners among the Federal soldiers generally, and in some instances among the officers. S. Hambright, Major and Provost-Marshal, with headquarters at the same place with General Gillam, was especially insulting to citizens, and cruel to the prisoners. Dr. Ballew, a

citizen of Lenoir, enfeebled and emaciated with con-
sumption, was arrested and carried to headquarters.
Feeling exhausted with the effort to walk there, he
sat down on the steps of the piazza, to await the
Major's pleasure. It was determined to send him to
prison, and he was ordered to get up and march, but,
from his feebleness, not being able to move quickly
enough to suit the chivalrous soldier, the Major, to
help him rise, stepped behind and gave him " *a rousing
kick.*" The citizens were heartily cursed for taking
food to them. From Lenoir they were marched rapidly up to the top of the Blue Ridge; several gave
out, several who started from Salisbury died. They
were all urged forward with threats of death. A
Lieutenant Shotwell attempted to escape, but being
overtaken, surrendered. He was then shot down and left
on the roadside unburied. A Mr. Wilfong, who had
captured a straggler of Kirk's command, brought him
into Lenoir, not knowing the Federals were there.
The tables were of course turned, and he in his turn
became a prisoner, and was given in charge to his
former captive, who wreaked such cruel vengeance on
him that he died before reaching Greenville, Tenn.
All who reached Knoxville were sent to Camp Chase,
Ohio.

General Gillam deserves especial notice at the hands
of the historian. All concurrent testimony represents
him as most supercilious, insulting, and unfeeling.
His headquarters in Lenoir, were at Mr. Albert Hagler's. The family were all crowded off into one room,
while the gallant General and his staff appropriated

all the rest of the premises, including kitchen and stables.   To Miss Sarah Hagler, an accomplished young
lady, he was especially impertinent, though she parried
his attacks with the civility of a lady.   On one occasion he said to her rudely, " I know you are a rebel
from the way you move—an't you a rebel?"   She
replied, " General Gillam, did you ever hear the story
of the tailor's wife and the scissors ?"   " Yes."   " Then
I am a rebel as high as I can reach."   Coarseness,
however, can not always be met playfully, and Mrs.
Hagler incurred his anger to its fullest extent when,
in reply to his violent denunciation of the Confederates
for starving their prisoners, she ventured to suggest
that the Federal authorities might have saved all this
suffering had they agreed to exchange and take them
North, where provisions were plenty.   The General's
reply to this was the giving his men tacit license to
plunder and destroy the houses of Mrs. H.'s married
daughter and niece, who lived very near her, and who,
she had supposed, were to be protected, from his headquarters being at her house.   No houses in the place
suffered more severely than theirs.   The house of her
daughter, Mrs. Hartley, was pillaged from top to bot-
tom.   Barrels of sorghum were broken and poured
over the wheat in the granary, and over the floors of
the house.   Furniture and crockery were smashed,
and what was not broken up was defiled in a manner
so disgusting as to be unfit for use.   Mrs. Clark, the
niece, was driven out of her house by the brutality of
her plunderers.   Her husband, Dr. Boone Clark, was
a captain in the Confederate service, had been wound-

ed in the battle of Leesburg, early in the war—an admirable and most graphic account of which engagement he wrote for the Raleigh *Standard* soon after. In several subsequent battles he had received severe wounds, and though partially disabled by one of them at this time, he was endeavoring to raise a company of cavalry for home defense, as marauders, under the notorious Keith and Blalock, were constantly threatening to pillage Lenoir. These facts were known to some of Gillam's men, and they evidently enjoyed the opportunity to plunder his house and insult his defenseless wife. He himself was at home, sitting at table, when the raiders dashed in town. Seizing his gun, he ran out and secreted himself behind some adjoining buildings, and though a colonel did him the honor to enter his house almost immediately, and with a squad made a thorough search for him, his retreat remained undiscovered, and at night he left for more secure quarters. The raiders swarmed through the house that evening and night, breaking open trunks, wardrobes, drawers; searching for arms and carrying off all the valuables, and destroying what they did not want. Finding a coat of the Captain's, they cut it to pieces. They destroyed all the provisions, all the furniture, crockery, and wearing apparel. They tore up fine silk dresses into ribbons for their hats, or cut large squares out and carefully wrapped up quids of tobacco in them and deposited them on the mantel-piece. The little daughter's hat and garments were placed on the floor, and loathsomely polluted. They even took the lady's thimble from her work-box, and carried off the likeness of her deceased mother, paying no regard to her entreaties. They constantly addressed her, as she sat weeping and motionless amid the wreck they were making, in the most profane and obscene and insulting language, repeatedly calling her a liar and other degrading names. They compelled her and her little daughter to remain and witness the destruction; and, finally, when there was nothing more to break and steal, one of them approached her and thrust his fist in her face. As she raised her head to avoid it, he struck her forehead, seized her by the throat, cursing her furiously. She begged him not to kill her; he let her throat loose then; seizing the neck of her dress, tore it open, snatched her gold watch, which hung by a ribbon, tore it off and left her. Half dead with fright, she rushed to the door with the child, and amid curses and cries of " Stop her !" "Don't let her go !" got out of the house, ran down to her aunt's, and fell fainting on the threshold. After she was recovered, the ladies begged General Gillam to interfere, but he refused, saying, " There were bad men in all crowds." In the case of Mrs. Hartley he turned his back to the ladies without a word. Mrs. Clark then appealed to Lieutenant Jerome B. Rice of the Signal Corps, and also to Lieutenant Theodore Mallobry in the same command. These were *gentlemen*, and manifested a determination to protect her. One of them returned to her house with her and viewed the utter destruction of her household property with every appearance of shame and indignation. As they entered the house a soldier — the last of the gang—ran out. The Lieutenant had him arrested and carried to headquarters. When Mrs. Clark was called on to identify him as one of the robbers, he denied having been near her house. "Why," said she, "that is a piece of a silk dress of mine round your hat now." "Is it?" said he, coolly taking it off and handing it to her; "well, then, you may have it back." This was in the presence of General Gillam, for whom, by the way, it was generally observed, the men seemed to have no respect. General Brown sent a strong guard to Mrs. Clark's house; but it was too late to save any thing, and she had no redress.

I have been thus particular to give an account which is, after all, a condensed one, of the treatment of *one* Southern lady by certain soldiers of the army of the Union. There are thousands of such cases unreported. This I present as a sample. So much is said of the "unharmonized" attitude of Southern women at present that I think it is as well to let the world see upon what ground it is they feel as if some time must elapse before they can honestly profess to love their enemies.

While plundering one house in the village, the marauders forced themselves into the chamber of a lady while she was in child-birth. With great difficulty the attending physician prevented them from plundering that room.

Mrs. General Vaughn was residing in Lenoir at this time. It is said that Generals Gillam and Vaughn had been friends before the war, and had agreed together that if the family of one should fall into the hands of the other, they should be protected. General Gillam placed a guard at Mrs. Vaughn's house; but as soon as

he left the town, two of his men went in and demanded
her watch. On her refusal they attempted to search
her. She drew a pistol, but they took it from her before she could fire. She resisted their search with all
her might, and at last they left her without the watch,
having nearly torn her dress off. Shortly after, the
same two returned with five others, and with threats
of violence compelled her to give the watch up. That
night squads of half-intoxicated men came back and
committed further depredations in the village and
neighborhood. The house of Dr. Felix Dula, with all
its furniture, was burned. This, however, it is con-
jectured, might have been done by deserters. They
left Lenoir for Morganton on the 17th, and on the way
burned the house of a Mr. Johnston, one of the home
guards. On reaching Rocky Ford, on the Catawba
river, a mile or two from Morganton, they found a
party of about fifty Confederates, strongly posted on
the opposite side, well· armed, and with one brass
howitzer. This party was under the command of
Captain George West, Lieutenant-Colonel S. M'Dow-
ell Tate volunteering with them. They were well
posted and sheltered on their side, while the enemy
approached without cover to attempt a very difficult
ford. A sharp engagement ensued, which resulted in
General Gillam's withdrawal toward Fleming's Ford,
a little higher up. He lost about twenty-five, killed
and wounded. Few were wounded. An eye-witness
says he counted eight dead bodies of Federal soldiers
floating down the stream. The Confederates lost none,
their position being so advantageous. At Fleming's

Ford General Gillam easily forced his way, the fifty Confederates taking to the mountains on finding themselves overpowered here.

The raiders remained at Morganton a day or two. There was very little plundering done in the houses here. They exercised their ingenuity in searching for hidden treasure out of doors. It seemed to have been understood that the Morganton people, warned of their approach, had *cached* most of their valuables. These *caches* were hunted up with unremitting vigor, and most of them were discovered and rifled. Many amusing stories are current now all through the South, of valuable deposits, scarcely hidden at all, which escaped, and some, not so amusing, of others hidden in inscrutable places which were pounced upon at once. Of a quantity of old family silver buried out of town, by a clump of rocks shaded with a persimmon-tree or two and a grape-vine, and on the departure of the enemy the owner going out and finding that a camp had been made just there, and the camp-fire built just over the *cache*, which was untouched. Of a valuable *cache* made by several families united, in a secluded spot in the woods, and found afterward undisturbed save by the hoof of a raider's horse having sunk in upon it, having evidently caused a stumble, but no suspicion of the cause. Of valuable papers and jewels so well hidden that it was months before the owners themselves could find where they had put them.

CHAPTER XVI.

PLUNDERING OF COLONEL CARSON—OF REV. MR. PAXTON—GEN-
ERAL MARTIN REPULSES KIRBY—GILLAM PLUNDERS DURING
THE ARMISTICE—OCCUPATION OF ASHEVILLE—WHOLESALE
PLUNDER—DISPATCH FROM GENERAL PALMER.

ON the road from Morganton to Asheville General
Gillam's men went through their usual programme,
wherever a house was to be plundered and ladies were
to be insulted and robbed! At Pleasant Garden one
of them, feeling that some clean linen was necessary
to his comfort, demanded a shirt of Colonel Carson.
The Colonel assured him that the house had been
thoroughly plundered, and the only shirt remaining to
him was the one he then had on. Having satisfied
himself of this fact, the soldier compelled the Colonel
(an old gentleman) to strip, and carried off his sole remaining shirt. I believe no officers were present at
the plundering of Colonel Carson's; but at the house
of the Rev. Mr. Paxton, an aged and amiable man, a
minister of the Presbyterian Church, officers were
present, and countenanced, if they did not directly aid,
the pillage. They carried off all that was portable,
even to knives and forks, and destroyed the rest of
the furniture. Having found some marmalade and

molasses, they made a mixture and smeared it over the bedroom furniture, etc.   Some of them locked Mrs. Paxton in her room, and attempted to torture her into the disclosure of hidden treasure, if she had such.   Her cries brought others to the door, and they desisted. Mr. Paxton's horse, watch, and all his clothing were taken of course.   Such were the rudeness and brutality which accompanied these robberies, that people were thankful to escape with their lives.

About the time that General Stoneman's return was expected in the West, a brigade of infantry, under command of a Colonel Kirby, was moved by the Federals from Greenville, Tenn., on Asheville, N. C.   It was supposed they would meet Stoneman there; but they arrived a little too soon, during the second week of April, and were met by the Confederates near Camp Woodfire, and so successfully repulsed that they turned about at once and returned to Greenville.

The troops by whom Kirby was repulsed were a part of the command of General J. G. Martin, referred to in our first chapter as the originator of the plan to furnish our soldiers through the blockade-runners. He was, as Governor Vance writes of him, a most gallant and efficient officer, especially valuable for the prompt energy which he infused into every department of business under his control.   When it was found that General Gillam intended to take Asheville, General Martin ordered his whole command, consisting of Palmer's brigade (composed of the Sixty-second, Sixty-fourth, and Sixty-ninth North-Carolina, and a South-Carolina battery) and Love's regiment of

Thomas's Legion, to the vicinity of Swannanoa Gap, on the road from Morganton to Asheville. Love's regiment was ordered to the Gap. They reached it before Gillam did, and after cutting down some trees, and making a few other arrangements to receive the raiders, waited their approach, and on their advance repulsed them without difficulty. General Gillam spent two days at this Gap, vainly endeavoring to effect a passage, and finally moved off in the direction of Hickory-nut Gap. Palmer's brigade was ordered to meet them there; but General Martin, giving an account of this affair, adds, "I regret to say the men refused to go." Rumors of General Lee's surrender and of Johnston's armistice were floating through the country, and men who fought bravely as long as there was hope were only too willing to lay down their arms at the first news of peace.

General Martin ordered the South-Carolina battery to Greenville, S. C., their horses being in too bad condition for active service. On its way it fell in with General Gillam, and was captured. On Saturday, twenty-second of April, General Martin received notice of General Johnston's armistice with Sherman, and immediately sent out two flags of truce, on different roads, to meet General Gillam. On Sunday afternoon he was met on the Hendersonville road, about six miles from Asheville. He agreed to abide by the truce, and requested an interview with General Martin, who accordingly, on Monday morning, twenty-fourth, went out to his camp. The interview resulted in an agreement that General Gillam should go through

Asheville to Tennessee, and that he should be furnished with three days' rations for his men, and that they would observe the truce. General Gillam, it should be remarked, upon the testimony of his own officers, had had official information of the armistice while at Rutherfordton, on his way from Swannanoa. But, nevertheless, he had continued the same system of depredation all along his route from Rutherfordton, sweeping the country of horses, mules, carriages, and property of every description, and destroying what they could not take along. On the twenty-fifth, General Gillam arrived in Asheville. Perfect order was observed. The nine thousand rations required were duly issued to him. General Gillam and his staff dined with General Martin; and as he was about to mount his horse to join his command, in the evening, General Martin asked him if he would give *him* the forty-eight hours' notice provided for in the truce, before renewing hostilities. General Gillam replied, "*Certainly— that the notice should be given.*"

That night General Gillam left his command encamped not far from Asheville, and went on to Tennessee. During the day, while the Federals were coming in, a party of officers dashed into town from the French Broad road, in a state of very apparent excitement. This was the notorious Colonel Kirke and his staff, who had approached at the head of two regiments for the openly avowed purpose of plundering Asheville, having heard of the dispersion of the Confederates from Swannanoa, and feeling sure of their prize at last. But finding the town quietly

occupied by General Gillam, under the terms of the
armistice, they expressed deep disappointment, and
swore roundly they would yet return and lay it in
ashes.   Now they were compelled to leave in advance
of General Gillam.*   The Federal army led in its rear
an immense train of plunder—animals of all sorts,
and carriages and wagons piled with property—household goods and treasures.   One load, however, was of
questionable value, being no less than fifteen negro
babies, the mothers marching in the crowd.   The
Asheville people had the mortification of seeing the
guns of the South-Carolina battery, just captured,
driven through by negroes.   Not a citizen was visible
in the streets; doors and windows were all closed;
but I have the best authority—that of a lady—for saying that from behind curtains and blinds many a glance
was shot from bright eyes, of contempt and hatred, on
the blue jackets.   Such lightning, however, is unfor-
tunately innocuous, and not known to produce fatal
effects outside of romances ; and so the raiders lounged
carelessly about, or sat down on the street-corners and
played cards, while waiting for their rations, in perfect
immunity from such electrical batteries.

Tuesday night passed quietly, and Asheville was
beginning to hope that hostilities suspended would

---

* Perhaps it is not generally known in North-Carolina that Colonel Kirke had
ardent aspirations for the provisional governorship of his beloved native State.
I saw a letter from him just after the break-up, in which he avowed this noble
ambition, evidently anticipating no very distant day when a grateful country
should reward his patriotism and gallantry.   By the way, it is said that Colonel
Kirke also is a native of Salisbury.   Both Kirke and Gillam !   I am afraid there
is a disposition to slander that fine old borough.

prove to be hostilities ended.   Our troops had almost
ceased to exist in an organized form.   The town was
guarded by only one company—Captain Teague's
scouts—besides General Martin and his staff, including
in all about thirty officers.   A small party of Federals
passed through during the twenty-sixth, under flag
of truce, carrying dispatches to General Palmer, who
was then approaching from Lincolnton by the Hickory-
nut Gap.   At sunset on the twenty-sixth, General
Brown, in command of a portion of the same troops
that had just passed through with Gillam, suddenly
reëntered the place, capturing all the officers and soldiers, and giving up the town to plunder.   The men
were paroled to go home, the officers·to report to General Stoneman at Knoxville.

This, be it remembered, was within twenty-four
hours after the above agreement with General Gillam,
on official news of General Sherman's armistice.

General Martin being arrested, was taken to General Brown, and after less than an hour's absence, was
permitted to return home in charge of a United States
officer.   On arriving at his house, he found the ladies
of his family, with lighted candles, going over the
house at the bidding of the marauders, lighting them
while they broke open doors, trunks, drawers, and
boxes, and helped themselves to what they chose.
And this was the experience of every house in the
place that night.   Many were entered by three or four
different gangs at once.   They swarmed in at every
avenue of entrance, generally by the back-door, having
taken counsel with the negroes first.   Mrs. Martin re-

covered some of her stolen goods by the assistance of a guard who was detailed after the house had been plundered. Not even the town of Fayetteville suffered more severely from pillage. Mrs. James W. Patton and her sister were both sick in bed. Their house was entered from front and back at the same time. The ladies' rooms were entered, they were dragged from their beds, their persons and the rooms searched, and their valuables taken. This was supposed to have been done upon the information of a servant, who had told that there were four watches in the house. Of these four watches, three were afterward recovered, through the agency of a Captain Patterson, Assistant Adjutant-General to General Gillam, who had been quartered at Mrs. Patton's, and who proved to be one of the few *gentlemen* in that division of the United States army.

Judge Bailey's family suffered as severely as any others, every thing portable of value being carried off, even to the boots from the Judge's feet. The wedding-rings of his wife and daughter were forced from their hands. Other ladies were stopped in the street and their jewelry forced from them. Those who applied to General Brown, who had the honor to command this extraordinary expedition, received no redress whatever. Dr. Chapman, a well-known and widely respected minister of the Presbyterian Church, was so entirely robbed of all his goods and valuables, that he had not a change of clothes left beside what he wore. The Tenth and Eleventh Michigan regiments certainly won for themselves in Asheville that night a reputation that should damn them to everlasting fame. No excuse was given for this violation of the armistice, except a lame story of their having been attacked by General Vaughn and returning to Asheville to revenge themselves. General Vaughn was at that time in Virginia. On Thursday, parties scoured the country in all directions, carrying on the work of plunder and destruction. On Friday, they left, having destroyed all the arms and ammunition they could find and burned the armory. On Friday afternoon, they sent off the officers they had captured under a guard. The town being left thus without arms or protectors, the citizens, remembering Kirke's threats, begged General Brown to leave a small force as guard; but he refused, saying, "They might take care of themselves."

On the twenty-eighth, the following dispatch from General Palmer—who was Brown's senior officer—to General Martin, released our officers and men from their parole, and set the disgraceful circumstance of their surprise and capture in its proper light, though not stigmatizing it as it deserved :

> HEADQUARTERS OF EAST TENN. CAV. DIV.,
> HICKORY-NUT GAP ROAD,
> April 28, 1865.

GENERAL : I could not learn any of the particulars of your capture and that of Colonel Palmer and other officers and men, at Asheville, on the twenty-sixth, and as our toops at that point were obliged to leave immediately, there was no time for me to make the necessary investigation.

I therefore ordered your release on a parole of honor, to report to General Stoneman.

On further reflection, I have come to the conclusion that our men should have given you, under all the circumstances, notice of the termination of the armistice, and that in honor we can not profit by any failure to give this notice. You will therefore please inform all the officers and soldiers paroled by General Brown under the circumstances referred to, that the parole they have given (which was by my order) is not binding, and that they may consider that it was never given.

Regretting that your brother officers and yourself should have been placed in this delicate position, I am, General, respectfully your obedient servant,

WILLIAM J. PALMER,
Brevet Brigadier-General Commanding.
General J. G. MARTIN, Asheville.

The citizens of Asheville also owed it to General Palmer's interference that two regiments of negroes, which had been sent over into Yancey county, and which were bearing down upon Asheville, (it was said, at the suggestion and with the concurrence of Kirke and Gillam,) for the purpose of plunder and arson, were countermanded and sent over into Tennessee.

The Asheville pillage concludes such accounts of General Stoneman's remarkable raid through Western Carolina as I have been able to collect. A rich harvest of incident yet remains for the future historian. I have done little more than indicate his route. Much of the above is taken verbatim from a MS. narrative furnished me, at my request, by Dr. R. L. Beall, of Lenoir, so admirably and accurately prepared that I hope it will be given to the public entire at no distant day. It gives me pleasure to acknowledge here my indebtedness to this gentleman, and my thanks for the generous public spirit he has displayed in his invaluable contribution to these pages.

CHAPTER XVII.

NOT till we had seen General Lee's farewell to his army, printed on a slip from the Danville *Register* office, and read in household circles with tears and sobs—not till then did we finally and fairly give up the Southern cause, and feel that it was indeed lost. That (for us) dismal fact once established, the large majority—I may say, the great body of Southern people—surrendered with their beloved and trusted leader. Here and there were doubtless some resolved still to blind themselves, to hope against hope, who talked wildly of collecting the scattered fragments of our armies, and prolonging the war beyond the Mississippi—or somewhere; but they were the exceptions, few and far between—*rari nantes*—who took counsel of their desperation rather than of their reason. For all men knew now, what had long been feared and suspected, that the ground on which we stood was hollow, and had given way hopelessly and forever, and that now we were to pay the reckoning of our four years' madness.

If North-Carolina had, through her Executive, anticipated the final crash, and after the failure of the peace mission to Fortress Monroe, had endeavored to treat separately with the United States Government, and be the first to tender her submission, (as there were some who would fain have had her try the experiment,) if our State had taken this step, four generations would not have heard the last of it. The whole failure of the cause would in time have been attributed to the treachery and faint-heartedness of Old Rip, as there are even now those who say it was the croakers who ruined us, and that Generals Lee and Johnston should not have surrendered so lightly. Besides the infamy, we should have gained *absolutely nothing*, as is plainly indicated by the course pursuing and pursued of the United States Government.

Governor Graham, as our representative in the Confederate Senate, and from his position, high *prestige*, and extended reputation, commanding the entire confidence of our people, might very well recommend that some steps should be taken, *if possible*, to avert the approaching crash, and spare the State the horrors of military subjugation. This it was his duty to do ; for to him more than any other man in the State, our people looked for guidance, and for some indication of the policy proper to be pursued in circumstances so critical and so desperate. But if Governor Vance had moved in the matter of sending commissioners to General Sherman one week sooner than he did, or had taken one step looking toward reconciliation, or submission, or negotiation, at any time previous to the second week of April, 1865, he would in all probability have been arrested by our military authorities as a traitor. There was positively nothing that with honor or credit could have been .done to meet the United States army sooner than it was done. Our affairs were at a dead-lock from the time of the adjournment of the Confederate Congress. Let those, therefore, who may yet be inclined to deplore that certain steps were not taken by our Executive, be satisfied that the course pursued was the only one possible. There is no room for misconstruction or misrepresentation in the future. Inaction in certain great and supreme moments is the highest wisdom, the truest dignity, as the Indian who finds his bark within the sweep of the rapids, and on the verge of the abyss, folds his arms and awaits the inevitable plunge with self-possession and calmness.

North-Carolina had nothing to retract, nothing to unsay, no pardon to beg. She had acted deliberately in joining the Southern cause. She had given her whole strength to it, with no lukewarm adherence; and now, in the hour of acknowledged defeat and failure, she did not attempt to desert, or abjectly bespeak any favors for herself on the ground of her anti-secession record or proclivities. And when the negotiations were completed and peace was finally announced, it would not be difficult to say what feelings most pre-dominated amongst us. We had desired peace—an end to the bloodshed and to the impending starvation of women and children. Peace we had longed and prayed for; but not *this* peace. The reünion was not *this* reünion. With all her former attachment to the old Union—with all her incredulity as to the stability or possibility of a separate independent Confederacy of the Southern States, even in case of its triumphant establishment—with all her sober conservative principles—I will venture to say, that there were not five hundred decent men within the limits of North-Carolina who could be found to rejoice in her military subjugation, or who, under such circumstances, welcomed the reäppearance of the Stars and Stripes as our national emblem. I have never yet seen one who did, or who was, at any rate, willing to avow it. At the same time, I must say, I have never seen one who evinced any intention of other than an honest acceptance of the situation, and a determination to do their whole duty and make the best of the inevitable.

Looking back at our delusions, errors, and miscalculations for the four years of the war, the wonder is, that the Confederacy lasted as long as it did. The last six months of its existence were indeed but mere outside show of seeming. That Richmond was doomed, was patent to all shrewd observers in the fall of 1864; and there was probably not a member of the Confederate Congress who did not know it when he took his seat at the beginning of its last session. It certainly reflects very little credit on the wisdom or the patriotism of that body that they did not, before adjourning, take some steps in concert to notify their respective constituents of their opinion as to the situation, and give some indication of the course they judged their States should pursue. Respect for President Davis, who was well known to be extremely averse to any movement looking toward reconstruction, and who refused to contemplate the event of our subjugation as possible—due respect for him may have influenced the extraordinary reticence of our Congress ; but it is more probable that an undue regard for their own political reputation and influence was the prime object with most of them. Whatever it was, history will point with a dubious expression to our representatives, each nudging his neighbor and desiring him to go forward—all convinced of the hopelessness of the cause, yet almost no man bold enough to say so publicly.

The Confederacy did not fail for want of genius to direct our military operations, nor for lack of the best qualities that go to make good soldiers in our armies, nor for lack of devotion and self-sacrifice among our people ; for they who most doubted the wisdom of our policy or of our success gave as freely as the most sanguine. The history of the rise and fall of the Confederate currency will be a singularly interesting and instructive lesson if it should ever be honestly written. Its steady, unchecked decline but too surely marshaled us the way we were going, and in the successive stages of its destruction we may read as in a mirror the story of our own facile descent.

After General Grant had succeeded in cutting the Petersburg Railroad, the authorities at Richmond looked with anxiety to the Deep River coal-fields in our State as the point where workshops could be located. Before that time there was but little interest felt or expressed in the struggle North-Carolina was making to get a road opened to them; but when the Richmond coal-fields were almost surrounded by the enemy, Chatham county, in our State, became an object of great interest to the Government. All the heads of departments were at once willing to lend a helping hand to the Raleigh and Chatham Coal-fields road. The iron from the Danville road, which had been taken up on account of the necessity of relaying that road with a more heavy rail, (taken from the Charlotte and Statesville road,) was granted to it, and a part of it was already on the way when Sherman arrived in Raleigh.

It is an interesting and suggestive fact connected with the want of transportation facilities in our last days, and showing the dire extremity to which we were reduced, that coal was carried from Deep River by rail and river past Fayetteville to Wilmington, thence by rail *via* Goldsboro, Raleigh, and Greensboro, to supply the government workshops in Salisbury and Charlotte. South-Carolina also sent trains for it to Wilmington. This coal was pronounced to be of the first quality, equal to the Cumberland coal, and one hundred per cent superior to the Richmond for blacksmith purposes. This want of transportation was one of the many stumbling-blocks in the way of the fainting Confederacy, and connected with the scarcity of provisions, and the strict military surveillance established in every district, brought many of us to the verge of starvation. Provisions were confined by military order to particular districts, each general taking care of his own. I have been told by Kemp P. Battle, Esq., our present State Treasurer, at that time President of the Raleigh and Chatham road, that on one occasion he was compelled—though he could have bought an abundance of provisions in Eastern Carolina—to send for bacon to South-western Georgia. He had to go to Richmond to see Secretary Seddon himself, and send an agent to General Beauregard at Charleston, in order to get permission to move it to North-Carolina. He was endeavoring on one occasion to get some corn for his own family up to Raleigh from his plantation in Edgecombe county, when the general in command of that department seized it, and in reply to application for it said, "If the owner is in the field, he may have his corn; if otherwise, not." In this connection what were called "the bonded plantations" were a curious institution in those latter days, which greatly added to the distress of our non-producers. For instance, the owner of a large estate with slaves, in order to keep an overseer out of the army to attend to it, gave bond with good security to deliver to the Government, or to soldiers' families, all his surplus produce at Government prices. By this arrangement of course our large planters could only sell their produce at much below the market price, and in fact for almost nothing, considering the value of our currency. And even this the Government did not pay. It died in debt to many: to Mr. Battle for nearly his whole crop of 1864. With great difficulty he got from a quartermaster, in March, 1865, six thousand dollars, which he immediately exchanged for fifty-seven dollars in gold. Besides this the Government impressed half the working mules, a source alone of no little vexation and distress among our small farmers. Our quartermasters were not always fair in their assessment, nor competent to decide.

The difficulties in the way of procuring provision can hardly be imagined by any but those who lived through that time. One of the last resorts was to smuggle cotton to the Chowan country in exchange for bacon, pound for pound. The greatest irregularities, of course, prevailed in different parts of the South. In some of the central counties of the Gulf States provisions were almost a drug in the market, (there being no transportation,) while here and in the army we were starving.

One of the last desperate expedients of our Government, and which bore as hardly on our people as any other, was the calling out of men between the ages of forty-five and fifty, and the Junior Reserves, mere children who should have been at home with their mothers. When the heads of families were taken away, often leaving a houseful of girls only to assist the mother to make bread, the distress and trouble were most piteous. At first the Government was inclined to be liberal in exemptions, but in the last ninety days all were taken.

On some counties of our State there was a disposition to resist or evade this wholesale conscription, and there were in consequence many deserters, many of whom lived by plundering their neighbors, and thus added to the general confusion and anxiety and peril of the times. Many acts of violence were committed in certain localities. Their expedients to escape capture, the modes of living they resorted to, the singular hiding-places they improvised or elaborated, would make an amusing and curious chapter in the history of the war—only these are the points which historians who desire to represent a people as unanimous in a great national struggle for rights and liberty do not generally care to present. If any of the immortal three hundred faltered on the way to Thermopylæ we have never been told of it. I know that we were greatly mortified to hear the stories that were told by those who were sent in search of our recreants. It was a severe shock to our high-strung thories of Southern chivalry and patriotism, to think of Southerners hiding in dens and caves of the earth, resolved with great constancy NOT to be martyrs, having to be unearthed in these burrows and dragged out to the fight. One warrior lived for weeks in a hollow tree, fed by his wife; another was conscripted from beneath his own hen-house, where he had dug out a sort of grave, into which, well supplied with blankets, he descended in peace every morning. One took possession of an old, deserted, and forgotten mine in his neighborhood, and by a skillful disposal of brush and rubbish at the entrance, kept house quite comfortably for months, plying his trade of shoemaker meanwhile, and supplied with food from home. The women, in such cases, were the instigators of the skulking. One soldier returning to his regiment, after

a furlough at home in a certain county, said, " He'd be
d—d if Jeff Davis wouldn't desert too if he were to
stay at —— awhile."

The history of our personal privations, our household expenses, our public donations, and our taxes,
will be a curious study of domestic and political economy combined.   People who before the war had lived
up fully to incomes of two thousand dollars a year,
were reduced to less than one tenth of that sum, and
are fully qualified now to give an answer to the question of how little one can live on.   Fifty dollars in
gold would have been gladly taken in exchange for
many a whole year's salary in Confederate currency
for the last year or two.   Even now it is an expli-
cable mystery to me how people with moderate salaries lived who had families to feed and clothe.   It was
done only by confining themselves strictly to the most
common and coarsest articles, and by an entire renun-
ciation of all the luxuries and most of the comforts of
life.   When tallow was thirty dollars per pound, people necessarily sat in darkness.   I have walked from
end to end of our town at night and not observed half
a dozen lights.   If we did not realize Charles Lamb's
notion of society, as it must have existed before the
invention of lights, when people had to feel about for
a smile, and handle a neighbor's cheek to be sure that
he understood a joke, it was because lightwood-knots
were plentiful, and turpentine easy of access.

The condition of the press was a striking commentary on the state of things among us.   Some pains
have been taken to secure an accurate list of our State

papers from an entirely reliable source. At the commencement of the war there were but two daily
papers in the State ; at the close, there were four in
the city of Raleigh alone. Of fifty-seven papers in
existence in May, 1861, twenty-six ceased during the
war. There are thirty-three now in the State, of
which ten are dailies. People who had never taken
more than their own county weekly in all their lives,
found the Richmond dailies a necessity during the
war, so great was the general anxiety to have the latest news, and above all from the army. The post-
offices were besieged for the dingy half-sheets that
came freighted with momentous intelligence for us.
The *Fayetteville Observer* and the *North-Carolina
Presbyterian* were the only two papers in the State
whose dimensions were not reduced to a half-sheet.
The *Fayetteville Observer* had been for forty years
one of the most ably edited, most sterling, and most
influential journals in the State, and I may add, in the
whole Southern country.* Its influence for good all
through that long period can hardly be overrated.
The editor, E. J. Hale, was an old-line whig in politics—a conservative of the strictest sort. His paper
ranged side by side with the *National Intelligencer;*
the *Richmond Whig,* and the other noble old journals of that school which had stood as breakwaters for
more than a generation against the incoming tide of
radicalism North and South, but were swept away at

* The writer might have added—or in America. Its editor, Mr. Hale, is a
gentleman of broad intellect, large information, and rare journalistic ability.—
ED. WATCHMAN.

last in the great flood. Mr. Hale opposed the doctrine of secession, and resisted its movement as long
as it was possible to do so. Mr. Lincoln's call for
seventy-five thousand men to coerce the South first
aroused his opposition to the United States Government; and after this State had gone over he supported her Act, and supported the war with all his power,
giving his sons, giving most liberally of all his substance, and dévoting his paper enthusiastically to the
benefit of the army, and the upholding of the State
and general government. For though no admirer in
past times of Mr. Davis's record as a Democrat poli-
tician, yet when he was elevated to the post of President of the Confederacy, and became the representative of the Southern people, no man gave him a more
generous support. His paper was published weekly
and semi-weekly without intermission, and with a constantly increasing circulation and influence, until the
appearance in Fayetteville of General Sherman's army,
on the twelfth of April, 1865, when the office was entirely destroyed, and the fruits of a lifetime of labor
scattered to the winds. The office of the *North-Carolina Presbyterian* was also destroyed at the same
time.

The *Raleigh Standard*, edited by W. W. Holden,
was for many years the leading organ of the Demo-
cratic party in the State; indeed it may be said to
have been the creator and preserver of that party, and
was perhaps the most widely-circulated and influential
of all our journals, for its reputation was not confined
to the State. It was edited with marked ability by a

man, unsurpassed as a party tactician, who thoroughly understood his business, and who always kept his powder dry. ·During the first two years of the war all parties seemed melted down and fused into one by the general ardor and excitement of the times; and our heretofore antagonist papers presented a most edifying spectacle of concord and agreement. In 1863, Mr. Holden seeing no prospect of a favorable end to the war by fighting, began to advocate a resort to negotiation upon the basis of possible reconstruction. This speedily rendered him obnoxious to those of us who desired the war to go on, preferring even military subjugation to peaceful reconstruction; while it drew more closely to his support those who desired peace on any terms. The state of feeling between these two parties came to be such that an internecine war among ourselves might have broken out at any time. It was excessively difficult and dangerous for our public men to move either way. A party of soldiers passing through Raleigh, in September, 1863, mobbed the *Standard* office, and the compliment was returned, by the friends of Mr. Holden mobbing the office of the war paper, conducted at that time by John Spelman, under the title of the *State Journal*. Mr. Holden deemed it prudent to suspend the issue of his paper for two months in the spring of 1864, in consequence of the passage of the act suspending the writ of *habeas corpus*—suspended also for a day or two on the arrival of General Sherman's army.

The *State Journal* changed hands and name in 1864. Under the title of *The Confederate*, and edited by Colonel D. K. McRae, it became the daily organ of the Confederate Government in this State, and continued to advocate the policy of our chief and the indefinite continuance of the war till within three days of General Sherman's entrance into Raleigh, when the office was entirely destroyed. It was edited with much spirit and ability, but with singular audacity and bitterness.

The organ of Governor Vance's administration was *The Conservative*, established in 1864 as a daily, and continuing till General Sherman's arrival, when it shared the fate of the *Confederate*, being utterly destroyed, except one small press, which General Slocum carried away with him. *The Progress*, daily, followed the lead of the *Standard* in politics, and like the *Standard*, was suspended for only a day or two on the occupation of Raleigh. It had the reputation of being the earliest and sprightliest retailer of news— generally ahead of its competitors in that department. All these, as well as all others in the Confederacy, with a few exceptions, were printed on half-sheets of exceedingly dingy paper, and their price ranged from twenty-five dollars to fifty dollars for six months. No subscriptions were taken for a longer period, in consequence of the steady decline in value of our currency. The typography and general appearance, to say nothing of their matter, would have rendered them objects of curiosity in any part of the civilized world, and afford a close resemblance to the journals published in the days of the Revolution of 1776. Such was the scarcity of paper among us, that they disappeared as fast as they were received; and a complete file of one of our Confederate papers, which would be an invaluable possession for an historical society fifty years hence, is probably even now an impossibility.

All literary influences were of course greatly checked and straitened, while our people held their breath in suspense as to the issue of the war. Colleges were closed, schools went on lamely for want of teachers, who were in the army, and for want of text-books. An effort was made here and there to supply the increasing demand for grammars, arithmetics, readers, and primers; but the paper was coarse and dark, and the type was old and worn—the general getting up of these home-made books affording the clearest evidence of the insurmountable difficulties under which our people labored in endeavoring to make books while struggling for bread. Some of them ran the blockade, being sent abroad to be stereotyped. Some of them need only a new dress to take their place as standards in any school in the country now; but the majority of them may be set down as failures. The common-schools, kept going at first, shared at last in the general decline and relaxation of order, and were hardly in existence at all at the close. As to books from abroad—magazines, papers, etc.—it may well be imagined that in the interior of the Confederacy at least, we were at a standstill in regard to all such means of improvement or information. Occasionally a copy of the *London Times*, or one or two of the leading New-York journals found its way from Richmond, or Wilmington, or Charleston, and was sent from house to house until utterly worn out. Occasionally some enterprising publishing house, getting hold of a copy of the latest English· novel, would issue a reprint of it, solitary copies of which circulated through a county, and soon shared the fate of the papers. Northern magazines or books were but little in request, and little read if obtained.* I am by no means certain that the loss of the current "light literature" of the day was a loss much to be deplored. Such privations may rather be classed among the benefits of the war.

* But one number of *Harper's Magazine* was seen at Chapel Hill during the war; this ran the blockade from Nassau : and one number of the *London Quarterly Review*, found among the effects of Mrs. Rosa Greenhow, which floated ashore from the wreck in which she perished. Among such of her books as were recovered, much damaged and stained with sea-water, was her narrative of her imprisonment in Washington, just published in London, and the MS. of her private journal kept during her visit to London and Paris. Her elegant wardrobe was sold at public sale in Raleigh, by order of the Confederate Government, for the benefit of her daughter in Paris.

CHAPTER XVIII.

As to the State University, perhaps more. than a mere reference to its condition at the close of the war may not unjustly form part of a contribution to our State history, since its influence and reputation have been second to those of no similar institution in the country, and its benefits have been widely diffused through every State of the Confederacy. Its Revolutionary history is not uninteresting in this connection. At the very time when all our State interests lay prostrate and exhausted from the Revolutionary struggle, the very time when a superficial observer would have thought it enough for the people to get bread to eat and clothes to wear, our far-seeing patriots, who knew well that without education no state can become great, and that the weaker we were physically the more need there was for intellectual force and power to enable us to maintain our stand among the nations—these wise men projected and laid the foundations of a State literary institution, which, uncontrolled and uncontaminated by party politics or religious bigotries, should be an honor and a benefit to the commonwealth through all future generations. General Davie may be said to have been the father of the University, though every man of distinction in the State at that time manifested a deep and cordial interest in its establishment.

Most of my readers are sufficiently familiar with the history of the State to be aware that, before the Revolution, the mother country would permit no college or university or school to be established but upon certain conditions utterly repugnant to principles of civil and religious liberty. The charter of Queen's College, at Charlotte, Mecklenburg county, (the college, town, and county, all three being named in loyal compliment to his queen,) was disallowed by George III., because other than members of the Established Church of England were appointed among the trustees. This act of tyranny did more to arouse the revolutionary spirit than the Stamp Act and all other causes combined. The money that belonged to the common-school fund was squandered by the mother country in the erection of a palace for the royal governor—the most splendid edifice of the time on the continent. And at the close of the war for independence, so impoverished was the country that the General Assembly could contribute nothing toward the establishment of the University, beyond endowing it with doubtful debts, escheats, and derelict property. So that if aid had not been given from private sources, it would never have struggled into existence. At the first meeting of the trustees, Colonel Benjamin Smith, the aid-de-camp of General Washington and subsequent Governor of the State, made a donation of twenty thousand acres of Chickasaw lands. Major Charles Girard, who had served throughout the perils of the war, childless in the providence of God, adopted the newly-born University, and bestowed on it property supposed to be equal in value to forty thousand dollars. General Thomas Person, the old chief of the Regulators, gave in cash ten hundred and twenty-five dollars* to the completion of one of the buildings; and Girard Hall, Person Hall, and Smith Hall, preserve in their names the grateful remembrance of the earliest and most munificent patrons of the institution. It is a striking evidence of the poverty of the times that the ladies of the chief city of North-Carolina were able to present only a quadrant in token of their interest in the new undertaking, and the ladies of Raleigh a small pair of globes.

In 1795, the first student arrived, and from that day to this the whole course of the University has been one of great and steadily increasing reputation and usefulness. Dr. Joseph Caldwell was president from 1796 to 1835, (with the exception of four years, when Rev. Dr. Chapman presided,) when the Hon. David L. Swain was appointed his successor, and he still remains at the head, the oldest college president in the

---

* There was then, as now, no money in the country, and this was the largest cash donation ever received by the University.

United States, and one of the most successful.   It is a
remarkable fact, and one strongly illustrative of the
conservative tone of our society, and of our North-
Carolina people in general, that for the long period
of seventy years there have been virtually but two
presidents—that two of the senior professors have remained for forty years each, one of them occupying
the same chair for that whole period.   Another professor has held his chair for twenty-eight years, another for twenty-four, another for seventeen years.   I
doubt if any other college in the country can show a
similar record.   During the five years immediately
preceding the war, the average number of students
was about four hundred and twenty-five — a larger
number than was registered at any similar institution
in the Union except Yale.   The average receipts for
tuition exceeded twenty thousand dollars per annum ;
and it is another circumstance which probably has no
parallel in American colleges, that with a meagre endowment, the munificent patronage of the public enabled the authorities of the institution to make permanent improvements in the edifices and grounds, and
additions to the library and apparatus, amounting in
value, as exhibited by the reports of the trustees, to
the sum of more than a hundred thousand dollars !
This was effected by skillful financiering, and by giving
the faculty very moderate salaries, and is a striking
illustration at least of North-Carolina thrift and careful management.   Since 1837, moreover, the faculty
have been authorized to receive without charge for
tuition or room-rent, any native of the State possessed

of the requisite endowments, natural and acquired, whose circumstances may make such assistance necessary. About ten young men annually have availed themselves of this privilege, and these have in numerous instances won the highest honors of the University, and attained like distinction in the various walks of life. Two remarkable cases of this character, presented during the discussion of the proposition to extend temporary relief to the University, in the last General Assembly, must be fresh in the remembrance of many of my readers. In addition to the beneficence of this general ordinance, the two Literary Societies of the institution have each annually defrayed the entire expenses of one or more beneficiaries, during the time referred to, and these recipients of their bounty have rendered service and occupy positions of eminence and usefulness which offer the highest encouragement to perseverance in such benefactions. An account current between the State and the University for the past quarter of a century, will show the amount of the tuition and room-rent of those young men, added to the benefactions of the Societies, is greatly in excess of all the direct contributions for its support derived from the public authorities. Nay, more, that these sums, added to the hundred thousand dollars resulting from the net earnings of the institution, were quite equal in amount to the entire endowment now annihilated by the repudiation of the war-debt, and the consequent insolvency of the Bank of North-Carolina, in the stock of which more than the entire endowment was invested.

Can any other College in the United States say as much?

At the opening of the war, the ardor with which the young men rushed into the military service may be inferred from the fact that of the eighty members of the Freshman class, but *one* remained to continue his education, and he was incapacitated by feeble health from joining his comrades in the field. Five members of the faculty volunteered for the war; and those who remained in their chairs, being incapacitated by age or by their sacred profession from serving their country otherwise than as teachers, resolved to keep the doors of the University open as long as a dozen boys could be found amid the din of arms who might be able to profit by it. When conscription was resorted to, to fill up the depleted armies of the South, the trustees resolved to appeal to President Davis in behalf of the University, lest it should be entirely broken up by too rigid an enforcement of the law. The results were an important part of our State history during the war, and embodied facts which had a significant influence at the close.

"RALEIGH, October 8, 1863.

"At a meeting of the Board of Trustees of the University this day, present: His Excellency Governor Vance, President; W. A. Graham, Jonathan Worth, D. M. Barringer, P. H. Winston, Thomas Ruffin, J. H. Bryan, K. P. Battle, Charles Manly.

"*Resolved*, That the President of the University be authorized to correspond with the President of the

Confederate States, asking a suspension of any order or regulation which may have been issued for the conscription of students of the University, until the end of the present session, and also with a view to a general exemption of young men advanced in liberal studies, until they shall complete their college course.

" That the President of the University open correspondence with the heads of other literary institutions of the Confederacy, proposing the adoption of a general regulation, exempting for a limited time from military service the members of the *two higher classes* of our colleges, to enable them to attain the degree of Bachelor of Arts.

" CHARLES MANLY, Secretary."

In accordance with this resolution, Governor Swain addressed the following letter to President Davis, which will be read with interest, as presenting some very remarkable statements in regard to the University and the village of Chapel Hill:

" UNIVERSITY OF NORTH-CAROLINA,
CHAPEL HILL, Oct. 15, 1863.

" *To His Excellency, Jefferson Davis, President of the Confederate States:*

" SIR: The accompanying resolutions, adopted by the trustees of this institution at their meeting in Raleigh, on the eighth instant, make it my duty to open a correspondence with you on the subject to which they relate.

" A simple statement of the facts, which seem to me to be pertinent, without any attempt to illustrate and enforce them by argument, will, I suppose, sufficiently accomplish the purposes of the trustees.

"At the close of the collegiate year 1859–60, (June seventh, 1860,) the whole number of students on our catalogue was four hundred and thirty. Of these, two hundred and forty-five were from North-Carolina, twenty-nine from Tennessee, twenty-eight from Louisiana, twenty-eight from Mississippi, twenty-six from Alabama, twenty-four from South-Carolina, seventeen from Texas, fourteen from Georgia, five from Virginia, four from Florida, two from Arkansas, two from Kentucky, two from Missouri, two from California, one from Iowa, one from New-Mexico, one from Ohio. They were distributed in the four classes as follows: Seniors eighty-four, Juniors one hundred and two, Sophomores one hundred and twenty-five, Freshmen eighty.

"Of the eight young men who received the first distinction in the Senior class, four are in their graves, (soldiers' graves,) and a fifth a wounded prisoner. More than a seventh of these graduates are known to have fallen in battle.

"The Freshmen class of eighty members pressed into the service with such impetuosity that but a single individual remained to graduate at the last commencement; and he in the intervening time had entered the army, been discharged on account of impaired health, and was permitted by special favor to rejoin his class.

"The Faculty at that time was composed of fourteen members, no one of whom was liable to conscrip-

tion. Five of the fourteen were permitted by the
trustees to volunteer. One of these has recently returned from long imprisonment in Ohio, with a ruined
constitution. A second is a wounded prisoner, now
at Baltimore. A third fell at Gettysburgh. The remaining two are in active field-service at present.

"The nine gentlemen who now constitute the corps
of instructors are, with a single exception, clergymen,
or laymen beyond the age of conscription. No one
of them has a son of the requisite age who has not entered the service as a volunteer. Five of the eight
sons of members of the faculty are now in active service; one fell mortally wounded at Gettysburgh, another at South-Mountain.

"The village of Chapel Hill owes its existence to
the University, and is of course materially affected by
the prosperity or decline of the institution. The young
men of the village responded to the call of the country
with the same alacrity which characterized the college
classes; and fifteen of them—a larger proportion than
is exhibited in any other town or village in the State—
have already fallen in battle. The departed are more
numerous than the survivors; and the melancholy
fact is prominent with respect to both the village and
the University, that the most promising young men
have been the earliest victims.

"Without entering into further details, permit me
to assure you, as the result of extensive and careful
observation and inquiry, that I know of no similar institution or community in the Confederacy that has
rendered greater services or endured greater losses

and privations than the University of North-Carolina, and the village of Chapel Hill.

"The number of students at present here is sixty-three; of whom fifty-five are from North-Carolina, four from Virginia, two from South-Carolina, and one from Alabama; nine Seniors, thirteen Juniors, fourteen Sophomores, and twenty-seven Freshmen.

"A rigid enforcement of the Conscription Act may take from us nine or ten young men with physical constitutions in general better suited to the quiet pursuits of literature and science than to military service. They can make no appreciable addition to the strength of the army; but their withdrawal may very seriously affect our organization, and in its ultimate effects compel us to close the doors of the oldest University at present accessible to the students of the Confederacy.

"It can scarcely be necessary to intimate that with a slender endowment and a diminution of more than twenty thousand dollars in the annual receipts for tuition, it is at present very difficult and may soon be impossible to sustain the institution. The exemption of professors from the operation of the Conscript Act is a sufficient indication that the annihilation of the best established colleges in the country was not the purpose of our Congress; and I can but hope with the eminent gentlemen who have made me their organ on this occasion, that it will never be permitted to produce effects which I am satisfied no one would more deeply deplore than yourself.

"I have the honor to be, with the highest consideration, your obedient servant,   D. L. SWAIN."

The result of this application was that orders were issued from the Conscript Office to grant the exemption requested. President Davis is reported to have said in the beginning of the war in reference to the drafting of college boys, that it should not be done; " that the *seed-corn* must not be ground up."

But as the exigencies of the country became more and more pressing, the wisdom of this precept was lost sight of. In the spring of 1864, in reply to a second application in behalf of the two lower classes, Mr. Seddon returned the following opinion to the Conscript Bureau:

" I can not see in the grounds presented such peculiar or exceptional circumstances as will justify departure from the rules acted on in many similar instances. Youths under eighteen will be allowed to continue their studies. Those over, capable of military service, will best discharge their duty and find their highest training in defending the country in the field.

" March 10, 1864."

In compliance with this opinion, the Conscript Act was finally enforced at the University; the classes were still further reduced by the withdrawal of such as came within the requirements of the act, or who were determined to share at all hazards the fate of their comrades in the army. The University, however, still struggled on; and when General Sherman's forces entered the place, there were some ten or twelve boys still keeping up the name of a college. The bell was rung by one of the professors, and morning and evening prayers attended to during the stay of the United States forces. The students present, with two or three exceptions, were those whose homes were in the village. The two or three who were from a distance, left on the advent of the Federals, walking to their homes in neighboring counties, there being no other means of locomotion in those days. But one Senior, Mr. W. C. Prout, graduated at the ensuing commencement, having taken the whole course. There were three others who received diplomas at the same time. For the first time in thirty years, the President was absent from these exercises, having been summoned by President Johnson to Washington City, to confer with him and with other North-Carolina gentlemen on the condition of affairs in the State. Not a single visitor from abroad attended the commencement, with the exception of some *thirty gentlemen dressed in blue*, who had been delegated to remain here and keep order. The residents of the village were the only audience to hear the valedictory pronounced by the sole remaining representative of his class. Where were the hundreds who had thronged these halls four years before ? Virginia, and Maryland, and Pennsylvania, and Tennessee, and Georgia were heaving with their graves ! In every State that had felt the tread of armies, and wherever the rough edge of the battle had joined, there had been found the foster-children of North-Carolina's University ;*

---

* It is stated upon good authority, and is confidently believed, that there was not a single regiment in the entire Confederate service in which could not be found one or more old students of Chapel Hill.

and now, sitting discrowned and childless, she might well have taken up the old lamentations which come to us in these later days more and more audibly across the centuries, " Oh ! that my head were waters, and mine eyes a fountain of tears, that I might weep day and night for the slain of the daughter of my people !"

There is not a prettier village in the South than that which lies around the University, and has grown up with it and has been sustained and elevated by it. And not a village in the South gave more freely of its best blood in the war, not one suffered more severely in proportion to its population.   Thirty-five of our young men died in the service.   Some of them left wives and little ones ; some were the only support and blessing of aged parents ; all were, with very few exceptions, the very flower of our families, and were representatives of every walk and condition of life. The first company that left the place in May, 1861, commanded by Captain R. J. Ashe, was attached to the famous First North-Carolina regiment, which so distinguished itself at the memorable battle of Bethel, June tenth of that year.   Upon the disbanding of this regiment, the members of the Orange Light Infantry attached themselves to other companies—for no fewer than four were raised here and in the vicinity—and many of them were among those who dragged themselves home on foot from Lee's last field.

The decline of the University threw many of our citizens out of employment, and the privations endured here tell as sad a story as can be met with any-

where. There was some alleviation of the general
distress for those who had houses or furniture to rent;
for every vacant room was crowded at one time by
refugee families from the eastern part of the State,
from Norfolk, and latterly from Petersburg. And
this was the case with every town in the interior of
the State. Some of these settled here permanently
during the war, attracted by the beauty and secluded
quiet of the place, and by the libraries—best society
of all! Some of them merely alighted here in the first
hurry of their flight, and afterward sought other
homes, as. birds flit uneasily from bough to bough
when driven from their nests. These families were
generally representatives of the best and most highly
cultivated of our Southern aristocracy. They fled
hither stripped of all their earthly possessions, except
a few of their negroes. Many came not only having
left their beautiful homes in the hands of invaders,
but with heads bowed down with mourning for gallant sons who had fallen in vain defense of those
homes. Some of them, the elders among them, closed
their wearied eyes here, and were laid to rest among
strangers, glad to die and exchange their uncertain
citizenship in a torn and distracted country for that
city which hath foundations.

The benefits of the war in our State should not be
overlooked in summing up even a slight record concerning it. It brought all classes nearer to each
other. The rich and the poor met together. A common cause became a common bond of sympathy and
kind feeling. Charity was more freely dispensed,

pride of station was forgotten. The Supreme Court judges and the ex-governors, whose sons had marched away in the ranks side by side with those of the day-laborer, felt a closer tie henceforth to their neighbor. When a whole village poured in and around one church building to hear the ministers of every denomination pray the parting prayers and invoke the farewell blessings in unison on the village boys, there was little room for sectarian feeling. Christians of every name drew nearer to each other. People who wept, and prayed, and rejoiced together as we did for four years, learned to love each other more. The higher and nobler and more generous impulses of our nature were brought constantly into action, stimulated by the heroic endurance and splendid gallantry of our soldiers, and the general enthusiasm which prevailed among us. Heaven forbid we should forget the good which the war brought us, amid such incalculable evils; and Heaven forbid we should ever forget its lessons—industry, economy, ingenuity, patience, faith, charity, and above all, and finally, humility, and a firm resolve henceforth to *let well alone*.

That North-Carolina has within herself all the elements of a larger life and hope, and a more diffused prosperity than she has ever known, is not to be doubted by those who are acquainted with the wealth of her internal resources and the consummate honesty, industry, and resolution of her people. Time will heal these wounds yet raw and bleeding; the tide of a new and nobler life will yet fill her veins and throb in all her pulses; and taught in the school of adversity the noblest of all lessons, our people will rise from their present dejection when their civil rights have been restored them, and with renewed hope in God will go on to do their whole duty as heretofore. Silently they will help to clear the wreck and right the ship; silently they will do their duty to the dead and to the living, and to those who shall come after them; silently and with the modesty of all true heroism they will do great things, and leave it to others to publish them. Remarkable as North-Carolinians have ever been for reticence and sobriety of speech and action, it is reserved for such epochs as those of May twentieth, 1776, and May twentieth, 1861, and for such great conflicts as succeeded them, to show what a fire can leap forth from this grave, impassive people—what a flame is kindled in generous sympathy, what ardor burns in defense of right and liberty. They are now to show the world what true and ennobling dignity may accompany defeat, surrender, and submission.

I close these slight and inadequate sketches of a memorable time with the words of my first sentence. The history of the great war is yet to be written, and can scarcely be fairly and impartially written by this generation. But it is our imperative duty to ourselves and to our dead to begin at once to lay up the costly material for the great work. Every man should contribute freely according to his ability, gold and silver, precious stones, iron and wood; and with this motive, I have ventured to present such an outline of events in the last ninety days as circumstances would permit me to gather.

APPENDIX.

---◆---

I.

" *More than a seventh of the aggregate number of graduates are known to have fallen in battle.*"

This was written in October, 1863. When the war was closed, the proportion was much greater.

It is hardly consistent with the slight character of these sketches to enter deeply into questions of constitutional law, involving the rights of belligerents and insurgents in time of civil war. I had no intention of attempting more than a plain, unvarnished statement of facts; with some hope, i confess, that a faithful narrative of the losses and the sufferings of the vanquished might do something at least toward arousing a generous remorse and regret in the breasts of the victors. This volume will produce an effect altogether contrary to what is intended if it serves only to prolong the remembrances which excite sectional animosity.

The records of our literary institutions all over the South will be found especially valuable in making up the estimate of our losses on the battle-field; for they will show unerringly that it was the *best* blood of the South that was poured out like water; that her educated young men were the first to offer themselves in what they deemed a glorious cause, and were among the first to fall. And North-Carolina, in particular, may point with pride to her University for an example of patriotic devotion unsurpassed by any other institution in the South.

I had hoped to be able to exhibit in this Appendix a collection of statistical details in connection with our University, of a deep and melancholy interest ; and have taken much pains and made numerous inquiries to ascertain what proportion of the living Alumni had participated in the contest, and what number had fallen in battle. It is, however, impossible to accomplish this design at present, and a complete record, if it can ever be obtained, must be reserved for future publication. I must content myself with a general view in relation to the actors of one particular era ; judging by which we may form some estimate of the whole number of those, who, having enjoyed the best advantages of education, and representing the best classes of society, counted not their lives dear in the service of their country.

Let me here present one scene at the University as it occurred in the days when the Almighty was yet with us, when His candle shined upon our head, and our children were about us.

The annual commencement of 1847 was rendered a literary festival of unusual interest, by the attendance of President Polk, and the Secretary of the Navy, Judge Mason, both of whom were alumni of the University.

The commencement of 1859 was rendered no less memorable by the visit of President Buchanan, and the Secretary of the Interior, Hon. Jacob Thompson, who was not only a graduate, but had been at one time a tutor in the Institution. How vivid is the recollection of those scenes in the minds of all who witnessed them! How interesting and imposing the assemblage of all that could give dignity or influence to a State, or shed the light of beauty and grace on these venerable cloisters and schools of learning. In 1859, apprehensions of the permanency of the Union were beginning to be excited by symptoms of dissatisfaction in the neighboring States. Secretary Thompson, in reply to the welcome addressed to him at his reception in front of Governor Swain's residence, referring to these ominous indications, congratulated the assembly on the steadiness of attachment to the Union everywhere manifested by the people of his native State. He was applauded with a vehemence which gave

full assurance of the deep and universal loyalty of his hearers.
President Buchanan repeatedly expressed his pleasure at these
evidences of feeling which were reïterated whenever occasion
offered. How little did he, how little did any one, foresee what
changes a single year was to effect. On the evening preceding
commencement-day, President Buchanan appeared upon the
rostrum and performed an interesting part in the exercises. At
the request of the Rev. Dr. Wheat, the then Professor of Rhe-
toric, he delivered the prize awarded to the best English writer
in the Sophomore class, Eldridge E. Wright, of Memphis, Tenn.,
who afterward graduated with the highest distinction, and the
most flattering hopes and promises of future usefulness. He
fell, a captain of artillery, in defense of his battery at the battle
of Murfreesboro. The two eldest sons of Dr. Wheat both fell in
battle—one at Shiloh and the other in Virginia. Of the six college tutors then present but one survives. Of the crowd of trustees and distinguished North-Carolinians who surrounded that
rostrum, time would fail me to tell of the prostrate hopes and
darkened hearths ; but in brief, I may say, that of the four hundred and thirty young men then listening with intense eagerness
and prolonged applause to words of wisdom and affection from
their chief magistrate, more than a fifth, in less than five years,
fell in fratricidal strife on every battle-field from Pennsylvania to Texas. Could the curtain that in mercy vailed the future,
have been that day withdrawn, what would have been the emotions of the audience ? Could they have seen one hundred of
those four hundred and thirty gay and gallant boys lying in all
the ghastly and bloody forms of death on the battle-field ; a like
proportion with amputated limbs, or permanently impaired constitutions ; and all, with few exceptions, seamed with honorable
scars, would they not have recoiled horror-stricken from such a
revelation of war as it really is? What would have been the
effect on that veteran statesman could he have seen all this—
seen his friend and associate in the councils of the nation an
exile, wandering in foreign lands, and all the widespread havoc,
ruin, and woe of a four years' merciless war darkly curtaining

the broad and smiling land ? In the providence of God he was childless. How many fathers of that goodly throng have gone down to the grave sorrowing—for sorrow slays as well as the sword ; how many mothers, sisters, and wives refuse to be comforted, and long for the grave, and are glad when they find it !

I have selected the catalogue of 1859–60 referred to in the letter from Governor Swain to President Davis, as best calculated to show the results of the fearful change produced among us in the brief interval preceding the civil war.

The Senior class of 1860 consisted of eighty-four members. The subjoined table will show that every one of these able to bear arms, with perhaps a single exception, entered the service, and that *more than a fourth* of the entire number now fill soldiers' graves. The proportion of the wounded to the killed is ordinarily estimated as not smaller than three to one ; and judging by this rule, it appears and is believed to be the fact, that very few of the whole class remained unscathed. Of the younger classes, my information is not sufficiently complete to justify the giving a list ; but enough is ascertained to make it certain that the sacrifice of life among them was in very nearly the same proportion as among the Seniors. As a matter of undying interest to the people of my own State, and significant enough to those of others, I present this record of the sons of her University.

Adams, Robert B. In service from South-Carolina.
Alexander, Sydenham B., Capt. 42d N. C. Regt.
Anderson, Lawrence M., Lieut. Killed at Shiloh.
Askew, George W., Capt. Miss. Regt.
Attmore, Isaac T. Killed in Virginia.
Baird, William W., Lieut. N. C. Regt.
Barbee, Algernon S., Lieut. Com. Dept. Army of the West.
Barrett, Alexander, Lieut. 49th N. C. Regt.
Battle, Junius C. Killed at Sharp's Mountain.
Bond, Lewis, Chief Ord. to Gen. Jackson.
Borden, William H., Lieut. 50th N. C. Regt.
Bowie, John R., Sergt. Signal Corps, Louisiana.

Brickell, Sterling H., Capt. 12th N. C. Regt. Resigned from wounds.

Brooks, William M., 3d N. C. Cav.

Bruce, Charles, Jr. Killed at Richmond.

Bryan, George P., Capt. 2d N. C. Regt. Killed.

Bullock, Richard A., Com. Sergt. 12th N. C. Regt.

Butler, Pierce M., 1st Lieut. 2d S. C. Cav.

Cole, Alexander T., Capt. 23d N. C. Regt.

Coleman, Daniel R., 20th N. C. Regt.

Cooper, Robert E., Chaplain Cobb's Legion.

Cooper, Thomas W., 1st Lieut. 11th N. C. Regt. Killed at Gettysburgh.

Daniel, S. Venable, 1st Lieut. 17th N. C. Regt.

Davis, Samuel C., Lieut. 4th N. C. Regt.

Davis, Thomas W., Lieut. 8th N. C. Regt

Drake, Edwin L., Col. Tenn. Regt. Cav.

Fain, John H. D., Capt. 33d N. C. Regt. Killed at Petersburg, 2d April, 1865.

Ferrand, Horace, Louisiana Regt.

Fogle, James O. A., Medical Dept. Richmond.

Franklin, Samuel R. Died in service.

Garrett, Woodston L., Lieut. 8th Ala. Cav.

Gay, Charles E., Lieut. Miss. Artillery.

Graham, James A., Capt. 27th N. C. Regt.

Haigh, Charles, Sergt.-Major 5th N. C. Cav.

Hale, Edward J., Jr., Capt. A. A. G. to Gen. Lane.

Hardin, Edward J., Lieut. and Adjt. Conscript Bureau.

Hays, Robert B., Forrest's Cavalry.

Headen, William J., Lieut. 26th N. C. Regt. Killed.

Henry, William W., Capt. Artillery, Army of the West.

Hightower, Samuel A., 26th Louisiana Regt.

Holliday, Thomas C., Capt. A. A. G. to Gen. Davis. Killed.

Houston, R. Bruce B., Lieut. 52d N. C. Regt.

Jones, H. Francis, Lieut. A. D. C. to Gen. Young. Killed.

Jones, Walter J., Heavy Artillery. Afterward 40th N. C. Regt.

Kelly, James, Presbyterian clergyman.

Kelly, John B., 26th N. C. Regt.

King, William J., Medical Dept. Richmond.

Lutterloh, Jarvis B., Lieut. 56th N. C. Regt. Killed at Gum Swamp.

Martin, Eugene S., Lieut. 1st Battery Heavy Artillery.

Martin, George S., Capt. Tenn. Art'y. Killed by bushwhackers.

McCallum, James B., Lieut. 51st N. C. Regt. Killed at Bermuda Hundreds.

McClelland, James C. Died in 1861, in Arkansas.

McKethan, Edwin T., Lieut. 51st N. C. Regt.

McKimmon, Arthur N., Q. M. Dept. Raleigh.

McKimmon, James, Jr., Lieut. Manly's Battery.

Mebane, Cornelius, Adjt. 6th N. C. Regt.

Mebane, John W. Capt. Tenn. Artillery. Killed at Kenesaw Mountain.

Micou, Augustin, Lieut. and A. A. G. Drew's Battalion.

Mimms, Thomas S., Western Army.

Nicholson, William T., Capt. 37th N. C. Regt. Killed.

Pearce, Oliver W., 3d Regt. N. C. Cav.

Pittman, Reddin G., 1st Lieut. Eng. Dep.

Pool, Charles C.

Quarles, George McD. Died in service.

Ryal, Tims, Louisiana Regt.

Royster, Iowa, Lieut. 37th N. C. Regt. Killed at Gettysburgh.

Sanders, Edward B., Sergt.-Major 35th N. C. Regt.

Saunders, Jos. H., Lieut.-Col. 33d N. C. Regt.

Scales, Erasmus D., Capt. and Com. Sub. 2d N. C. Cav.

Smith, Farquhard, Jr., 3d N. C. Cav.

Smith, Norfleet, 1st Lieut. 3d N. C. Cav.

Smith, Thomas L. Killed at Vicksburgh.

Sterling, Edward G. Died in service.

Strong, Hugh. In South-Carolina service.

Sykes, Richard L. In Mississippi service.

Taylor, George W., Ass't. Surgeon, 26th La.

Thompson, Samuel M., Colonel Tenn. Regt.

Thorp, John H., Capt. 47th N. C. Regt.

Vaughan, Vernon H.   In Alabama service

Wallace, James A., 44th N. C. Regt.

Wier, Samuel P., Lieut. 46th N. C. Regt.   Killed at Fredericks-
    burgh.

Whitfield, Cicero, Sergt. 53d N. C. Regt.

Wilson, George L.   Died.

Wooster, William A., Capt. 1st N. C. Regt.   Killed at Richmond.

Of field-officers in the Confederate service, at least thirteen illustrious names are among the Alumni of the University, namely :

    Lieut.-General Leonidas Polk,

    Brig.-Generals Geo. B. Anderson,

               Rufus Barringer,

               L. O'B. Branch,

               Thomas L. Clingman,

               Robert D. Johnston,

               Gaston Lewis,

               James Johnston Pettigrew,

               Matt. W. Ransom,

               Ashley W. Spaight ; and

    Adjutant-Generals

               R. C. Gatlin,

               John F. Hoke.

Generals Polk, Anderson, Branch, and Pettigrew were killed,
and all the others (with the exception of the two bureau
officers) severely wounded, and most of them more than once.

I regret that my information in regard to many other gallant
field-officers is at present too imperfect to justify the enumera-
tion ; much less am I able to give a correct list of subaltern officers, and the unrecorded dead.   It will be a labor of love to continue my inquiries, in the hope of being able at some future day
to present a suitable memorial of all our loved and lost.

> Beloved till Time can charm no more,
> And mourned till Pity's self be dead.

In looking over the list of even so few as are recorded above, one is struck with the number of those killed, of whom interesting and touching obituary memorials might be written. Nearly all of them were men of rank. One of the most widely read and admired and useful religious biographies of the day has been Miss Marsh's Life of Captain Hedley Vicars of the English Crimean Army. We had many a Captain Vicars in our Southern Confederate army, whose life, if written as well, would be quite as striking, quite as valuable—many pure and noble Christian young men, the beauty of whose daily lives still sheds a glow around their memories. It was in fact a common remark, during the war, that it was the best who fell. I am sure that North-Carolinians, at least, will not be displeased with particular mention of a few of their dead in this place.

Of the six tutors connected with the University at the opening of the war, all of whom volunteered at once, *five*—namely, Captains Anderson, Bryan, Johnson, Morrow, and Lieutenant Royster —fell on the battle-field, and they were all, without one exception, young men of more than ordinary promise.

Captain Anderson, of Wilmington, was a brother of General George B. Anderson. He graduated with the highest distinction in the year 1858. His class consisted of ninety-four members, nearly all of whom it is believed entered the army. Two of the seven who shared the first distinction with him—one subsequently tutor in the University, W. C. Dowd, the other Captain W. C. Lord, of Salisbury—are in their graves.

Captain William Adams, of Greensboro, whose name occurs first on the roll of his classmates, was killed at Sharpsburgh. Captain Hugh T. Brown, (half-brother to General Gordon,) fell at Springfield ; and Lieutenant Thomas Cowan, at Sharpsburgh. Among those who have survived the perils of the battle-field and the hospital, are Lieutenant-Colonels H. C. Jones, A. C. McAllister, and J. T. Morehead, Colonels John A. Gilmer and L. M. McAfee, and General Robert D. Johnston.

Captain Anderson was a candidate for orders in the Episcopal Church, but believed it his duty to contribute his share to the vindication of the rights of his country. He served with continually increasing reputation, and fell in the battle of the Wilderness Creek.

Captain George Pettigrew Bryan, of Raleigh, was another most rare spirit. Belonging to the class of 1860, enumerated above, he was the youngest of eight who received the first distinction. During his college life, and throughout the whole of his brief but brilliant career, he was as conspicuous for his fidelity to duty as for his intellectual attainments. He, too, was to have consecrated his rare gifts to the ministry of the Church. He fell, while leading a charge on the enemy's works, ten miles east of Richmond. Mortally wounded in the breast, he said, " Boys, I'm killed, but I wish I could live to see you take those works." In a few moments the works were carried and the enemy routed. In half an hour after, he died peacefully and calmly : his promotion to lieutenant-colonel arriving just after his death.

Captain George B. Johnson, of Edenton, a graduate of 1859, bearing away the highest honors, died in Chapel Hill of a decline brought on by the hardships of prison life at Sandusky, Ohio. One of his professors wrote of him : " His powers of mind were unusual, his energy of character very marked, his tastes all scholarly, and his attainments extensive and accurate. Always pure and upright and truthful and unselfish. Never was a whisper of reproach or censure uttered against him."

Lieutenant I. Royster, of Raleigh, was one of the graduates of this University who would have shed a lustre on its name had he lived. One of the eight of 1860 who received the first distinction, he was in many respects a remarkable genius—intellectually one of the most gifted young men who ever left these halls. He fell at Gettysburgh, advancing to the charge considerably in front of his company and singing "Dixie" as he met his instant death.

Captain E. Graham Morrow, of Chapel Hill, fell at Gettysburgh. Another noble, modest, gallant, and true young man. He was a son of North-Carolina in a particular sense, for he came of fathers, grandfathers, great-grandfathers and ancestors even more remote who had been an honor to the same soil before him. On these six slight memorials there is yet a crown to be placed.

These young men were all Christians. That light above any that ever shone by sea or shore falls upon their graves.

In the list of the Seniors of 1860 given above, of the eight who received the first honors of the University, but three survive; of the *twenty-seven* distinguished (more than a third of the whole number) ten are no more. Of the twenty-four dead, who shall estimate the loss to their country, and to their families of even these? Of one of the fairest and best, Captain John Fain, of Warren, who was the only child of his mother, and she a widow; killed after passing safely through four years of peril and suffering, and falling in the last day of the last fight before Petersburg, April 2d, 1865. Another of the first eight was Junius C. Battle, of Chapel Hill, fourth son of the Law Professor, Judge Battle. Having suffered amputation of the left leg, after the battle of South-Mountain, he occupied such of the few remaining hours of his life as he could redeem from his own sufferings, in reading to the crowd of Confederate and Federal wounded around him. We can well imagine, wrote a friend, how eloquent such reading was to such an audience. The reader's own eye was fast glazing, and the pains of death among strangers were upon him, but he rallied the remnants of his vision and self-control, and spent them in directing the fading eyes around him to that WICKET-GATE and SHINING LIGHT. Surely it was a cup of cold water given in the name of his Master, and even now is abundantly rewarded.

Of William A. Wooster of Wilmington, and of George L. Wilson of New-Berne, of whom, standing before him to say farewell, Gov. Swain said that he never had under his care, never had known two young men of higher character, purer faith, or more gifted intellect than these two beloved pupils.

I am tempted to go on with this list, but am reminded that I shall exceed my limits. Some abler hand, I trust, will some day gather up for preservation all these records of our noble boys; worthy, all of them, of that glorious epitaph once to be seen at Thermopylæ: "Tell it in *North-Carolina*, that we lie here in obedience to HER laws."

Of our Generals much might be said that would be of deep and permanent interest. In General Pettigrew, North-Carolina was universally and justly considered to have lost one of the most remarkable men that this continent has ever produced. He graduated in 1847, when he and General Ransom received the first distinction in their class. The latter delivered the Salutatory of his class to President Polk, and fortunately survives the perils of many a battle-field still further to honor and receive honor from his native State. Of General Pettigrew I append a biographical sketch, which originally appeared in the *Fayetteville Observer*, by a hand fully competent to do him justice, and which presents him not overdrawn nor too highly colored. Of none of the thousands of the flower of this Southern land who fell in her defense can it be said more justly than of James Johnston Pettigrew:

"*Felix non solum claritatê vitæ, sed etiam opportunitatê mortis.*" *

* Fortunate not only in the renown of his life, but also in the opportunity of his death.

II.

GEN. JAMES JOHNSTON PETTIGREW.

From The Fayetteville Observer.

JAMES JOHNSTON PETTIGREW, late a Brigadier in the army of the Confederate States, was born at Lake Scuppernong, in Tyrrell county, North-Carolina, upon the 4th day of July, 1828. His family is originally of French extraction. At an early period, however, one branch of it emigrated to Scotland, where it may be traced holding lands near Glasgow about the year 1492. Afterward a portion of it removed to the northern part of Ireland. From this place James Pettigrew, the great-grandfather of the subject of this notice, about the year 1732, came into Pennsylvania, and, some twenty years afterward, into North-Carolina. About 1770, this gentleman removed to South-Carolina, leaving here, however, his son Charles, who was a resident successively of the counties of Granville, Chowan, and Tyrrell. Charles Pettigrew was subsequently the first Bishop-elect of the Protestant Episcopal Church in this diocese. He died in 1807, and his memory survives, fragrant with piety, charity, and an extended usefulness. His son Ebenezer succeeded to his estates and reputation. Devoting his life to the successful drainage and cultivation of the fertile lands which he owned, and to the government of the large family of which he was the head, Mr. Pettigrew resisted every solicitation presented by his neighbors for the employment of his talents in public service. Upon one occasion alone was his reluctance overcome. In 1835, he was chosen by a very flattering vote to represent his District in the Congress of the United States. At that election he received the rare compliment of an almost unanimous vote from his fellow-citizens of Tyrrell, failing to obtain but three votes out of more than seven hundred. He could not be prevailed upon to be a candidate at a second election. Mr. Pettigrew married Miss Shepard, a daughter of the distinguished family of that name seated at New-Berne. She died in July 1830, when her son James Johnston was but two years of age. Ebenezer Pettigrew lived until July, 1848, having witnessed with great sensibility the very brilliant opening of his son's career among the cotemporary youth of the land.

After his mother's death the child was taken to the home of his grandmother at New-Berne, and there remained until he was carried into Orange county, to pursue his education. Owing to an unfortunate exposure whilst an infant, young Pettigrew was a delicate boy, but by diligent and systematic exercise he gradually inured his constitution to endure without harm extraordinary fatigue and the extremes of weather. He was a member of various schools at Hillsboro from the year 1836, enjoying the advantages of instruction by Mr. Bingham for about four years previously to his becoming a student at the University. During this period the state of his health required him to be often at home for several months together. He was a member of the University of North-Carolina during the full term of four years, graduating there at the head of his class in June, 1847. From early childhood young Pettigrew had been noted as a boy of extraordinary intellect. At all the schools he was easily first in every class and in every department of study. He seemed to master his text-books by intuition. They formed the smallest portion of his studies, for his eager appetite for learning ranged widely over subjects collateral to his immediate tasks. Nor did they always stop here. His father was amused and gratified upon one occasion to observe the extent to which he had profited by his excursions among the medical books of an eminent physician at Hillsboro, of whose family he was an inmate at the age of fourteen. In the class-room at the University he appeared in reciting rather to have descended to the level of the lesson, than to have risen up to it. Student as he was, and somewhat reserved in demeanor, he was nevertheless very popular with his fellows, and the object of their enthusiastic admiration. Anecdotes were abundant as to the marvelous range of his acquirements, and the generosity and patience with which he contributed from his stores even to the dullest applicant for aid. Nor was it only in letters that he was chief. A fencing-master, who happened to have a class among the collegians, bore quite as decided testimony to his merits as he had obtained from the various chairs of the faculty.

The commencement at which he graduated was distinguished by the attendance of President Polk, Mr. Secretary Mason, and Lieutenant Maury of the National Observatory. Impressed by the homage universally paid to his merits, as well as by the high character of his graduating oration, these gentlemen proposed to him to become an assistant in the Observatory at Washington City. After spending some weeks in recreation, Mr. Pettigrew reported to Lieutenant Maury, and remained with him for some six or eight months. In the occupations of this office he fully maintained his earlier promise; but soon relinquished the position, inasmuch as the exposure and labor incident to it were injuriously affecting his health.

After an interval of travel in the Northern States, Mr. Pettigrew, in the fall of 1848, became a student of law in the office of James Mason Campbell, Esq., of Baltimore, where he remained for several months. At the close of this period, by the solicitation of his kinsman, the late James L. Petigru of Charleston, S. C., he entered his office with the design of being subsequently associated with him in the practice of his profession. Upon obtaining license, Mr. Pettigrew, by the advice of his kinsman just mentioned, proceeded to Berlin and other universities in Germany in order to perfect himself in the civil law. He remained in Europe for nearly three years. Two years of this time he devoted to study, the remainder he spent in traveling upon the Continent, and in Great Britain and Ireland. He availed himself of this opportunity of becoming acquainted with modern European languages so far as to be able to speak with ease in those of Germany, France, Italy, and Spain. During this tour he contracted a great partiality for the Spanish character and history, having had considerable opportunity for studying the former not only as a private gentleman, but also as Secretary of Legation for a short while to Colonel Barringer, then Minister of the United States near the Court of Spain. It may be proper to add here, that among the unaccomplished designs of Mr. Pettigrew, to which he had given some labor, was that of following Prescott in further narratives of the connection of Spain with America, and as a preliminary to this he had formed a collection of works in Arabic, and had made himself acquainted with that language.

Mr. Pettigrew returned to Charleston in November, 1852, and entered upon the practice of law in connection with his honored and accomplished relative He profited so well by his studies in Europe and by his subsequent investigations, that in the opinion of his partner, who was well qualified to judge, he became a master of the civil law not inferior in acquisition and in grasp of principle to any in the United States. His success at the bar was brilliant. In 1856, he was chosen one of the representatives of the city in the Legislature, holding his seat under that election for the two sessions of December, 1856, and December, 1857. He rose to great distinction in that body. His report against the reöpening of the Slave Trade, and his speech upon the organization of the Supreme Court, gave him reputation beyond the bounds of the State. He failed to be reëlected in 1858.

Mr. Pettigrew persistently refused to receive any portion of the income of the partnership of which he was a member. Independent in property, and simple in his habits of personal expenditure, he displayed no desire to accumulate money. Noble in every trait of character, he held the contents of his purse subject to every draft that merit might present.

For some years previous to the rupture between the North and the South, Mr. Pettigrew had anticipated its occurrence, and believing it to be his duty to be prepared to give his best assistance to the South in such event, had turned his attention to military studies. Like many other rare geniuses, he had always a partiality for mathematics, and so very naturally devoted much time to that branch of this science which deals with war. Even as far back as 1850 he had been desirous of becoming an officer in the Prussian army; and negotiations for that end set upon foot by military friends whom he had made at Berlin, failed only because he was a republican. Afterward he became Aid to Governor Alston of South-Carolina, and more recently to Governor Pickens. Upon the breaking out of the war between Sardinia and Austria, Colonel Pettigrew at once arranged his private business and hastened to obtain position in the army under General Marmora. His application to Count Cavour was favorably received, but after consideration his offer was declined on the ground that the event of the battle of Solferino had rendered further fighting improbable. He was greatly disappointed, as his reception had inspired him with hopes of seeing active service in the Sardinian army with rank at least as high as that of· a colonel.· Availing himself, however, of his unex-- pected leisure, he revisited Spain, and after a stay of a few months returned to South-Carolina. The fruits of this second visit were collected by him into a volume entitled Spain and the Spaniards, which he printed for the inspection of his friends in 1860. It will be found to be a thoughtful, spirited, and agreeable record of his impressions of that ·romantic land.

At the opening of the present war, Colonel Pettigrew, as Aid to Governor Pickens, took a prominent part in the operations of Charleston. He was at that time also colonel of a rifle regiment in which he was much interested, and which became conspicuous amongst the military organizations around Charleston in the winter of 1860–1861. As commander of this body he received the surrender of Castle Pinckney, and subsequently held himself in readiness to storm Fort Sumter, in case it had not surren-

dered after bombardment.   Later in the spring, having failed
to procure the incorporation of his regiment into the army of
the Confederate States, and believing there was little chance of
seeing active service in South-Carolina, he transferred himself
as a private into Hampton's Legion, and early in the summer
accompanied that corps into Virginia.   A few days afterward
he was recalled to the service of his native State by an unsolic-
ited election as Colonel of the 12th Regiment of North-Carolina
Volunteers, now the 22d Regiment of North-Carolina Troops.
It had been Colonel Pettigrew's earnest wish to become connected
with the North-Carolina army, and so he at once accepted the
honorable position, and repaired to Raleigh where his regiment
was stationed in its camp of instruction.   He devoted his attention to its discipline with great assiduity, and in the early days of
August was ordered into Virginia.   The fall and winter of 1861
were spent by him near Evansport, upon the Potomac.   He gave
his whole time and attention to the perfecting of his regiment,
in the duties of soldiers.   He fully shared in every hardship that
was incident to their situation.   In this new position Colonel Pettigrew became conspicuous for another characteristic necessary
to eminent success in every department, but especially in that of
military life.   The men under his command became devotedly
attached to him.   Their enthusiasm knew no bounds.   Their
confidence in his administration of the police of the camp was
perfect, and their assurance of his gallantry and skill unqualified.
He soon felt that he might rely upon his brave men for all that
was possible to soldiers, and his attachment to the regiment
became marked.   Being offered promotion to the rank of brigadier, he declined it on the ground that it would separate him from
his regiment.   Some time later in the spring of 1862, an arrangement was made by which the 12th Regiment was included in
the brigade that was tendered to him, and he no longer felt any
difficulty in accepting the promotion.

General Pettigrew shared in the march under General Johnston into the Peninsula, and afterward in the retreat upon Richmond.   On the 1st day of June, 1862, in the battle of Seven Pines,

he was severely wounded by a ball which passed transversely along the front of his throat and so into the shoulder, cutting the nerves and muscles which strengthen the right arm. This occurred in a charge which he had headed with great gallantry. He was left upon the field for dead, and recovered his consciousness only to find himself in the hands of the enemy. Some weeks later his exchange was effected, and, being still an invalid, he was placed in command at Petersburg. The exigencies of the service having required his regiment to be transferred to another brigade, he found, upon his return, that it had been placed under the gal-lant—and now, alas! lamented—General Pender. By degrees a new brigade assembled around General Pettigrew, and such was his pains in its instruction, and such the desire among the North-Carolina soldiers to make part of his command, that by the close of the year he was at the head of a brigade which, in point of quality, numbers, and soldierly bearing, was equal to any in the army. He commanded this brigade in repelling the Federal raid into Martin county, late in the fall of 1862, and again in General Foster's expedition against Goldsboro, in December, 1862, and although the quick dexterity of the enemy in falling back did upon neither occasion afford him and his associates an opportu-nity of trying conclusions with them, yet upon both occasions the magnificent appearance of Pettigrew's Brigade tended greatly to revive the spirit of a community recently overrun by the enemy. He was also with General D. H. Hill during the spring of this year, in his attempt upon Washington in this State; and in the very brilliant affair at Blount's Creek gave the public a taste of what might be expected from his abilities when untrammeled by the orders of a superior.

At the time of General Stoneman's raid on the north of Rich-mond, General Pettigrew was ordered to the protection of that city, and shortly afterward took position at Hanover Junction. His brigade subsequently made part of the Army of Northern Vir-ginia, and accompanied General Lee into Pennsylvania. At the battle of Gettysburgh he was in command of General Heth's di-vision, and won many laurels. His division was greatly cut up.

The loss of his brigade in killed and wounded was so heavy as almost to destroy its organization. He himself was wounded by a ball which broke one of the bones of his hand. He regarded it so little as not to leave the field. Moving afterward with General Lee to Hagerstown and the Potomac, it devolved upon General Pettigrew, on the night of the 13th and the morning of the 14th of July, to assist in guarding the passage of that part of the army which recrossed at Falling Water. About nine o'clock in the morning of the latter day, having been in the saddle all night, General Pettigrew and other officers had thrown themselves upon the ground for a few moments' rest, when a party of Federal cavalry rode into their midst. In the *mêlée* which ensued General Pettigrew was shot—the ball taking effect in the abdomen and passing through his body. When the enemy had been repulsed, he was taken up by his sorrowing soldiers and carried across the river some seven miles into Virginia, along the track of the army. Upon the next day he was carried some fifteen miles further, to the house of Mr. Boyd at Bunker Hill, where he received every attention of which his situation allowed. Upon General Lee's expressing great sorrow for the calamity, he said that his fate was no other than one might reasonably anticipate upon entering the army, and that he was perfectly willing to die for his country. To the Rev. Mr. Wilmer he avowed a firm persuasion of the truths of the Christian religion, and said that in accordance with his belief he had some years before made preparations for death, adding, that otherwise he would not have entered the army. He lingered until the 17th, and then at twenty-five minutes after six in the morning, died, quietly and without pain. The expression of sympathy for his sad fate was universal. Private soldiers from other commands and distant States, vied with his own in repeated inquiries after his condition. Upon its way to Raleigh his body was received by the authorities and by the citizens everywhere with all possible respect and attention. On the morning of Friday, the 24th of July, the coffin, wrapped in the flag of the country, and adorned with wreaths of flowers and other tributes of feminine taste and tenderness, lay in the rotunda of the Capitol, where, within the year, had preceded him his compatriots Branch and Anderson. Later in the day the State received his loved and honored remains into her bosom.

It was a matter of great gratification to North-Carolina when this son, after an absence of a few years, gladly returned to her service. She views his career in arms with a just pride. She will ever reckon him among the most precious of her jewels; and will hold him forth as the fittest of all exemplars to the coming generations of her young heroes. Chief among his triumphs will it be reckoned that in the midst of his elevation and of the high hopes which possessed his soul, he so demeaned himself as to secure a place, hallowed by grief, in many an humble heart throughout North-Carolina. His name is to be pronounced reverently and with tears by the winter fireside of many a hut; and curious childhood will beg to have often repeated the rude stories in which soldiers shall celebrate his generosity, his impartiality, his courtesy, and his daring. It is true that many eyes which flashed with enthusiasm as their favorite urged his gray horse into the thick of the battle, are forever dull upon the fatal hills of Pennsylvania; but this will render his memory only the more dear to the survivors; what of his fame was not theirs originally, they will claim to have inherited from the dead around Gettysburgh.

If this story has been properly told, little remains to be said by way of comment. A young man of very rare accomplishments and energy, fitted equally for the cloister of the scholar and for the field of battle, has been snatched from our midst. Admirably qualified to be of assistance to the country as a soldier or as a statesman, General Pettigrew has been suddenly removed at the very commencement, as it were, of his career.

> *Ostendent terris hunc tantum fata, neque ultra*
> *Esse sinent.*

Although what he has achieved is sufficient for fame, that which impresses the observer most forcibly is that such vast preparation should, in the course of Providence, be defeated of an opportunity for display at all commensurate with what seemed its reasonable requirements. Under the circumstances his death looks like a prodigious waste of material. It adds a striking illustration to that class of subjects which has always been popular in poetry, and in morals whether heathen or Christian. It appears very clearly that the Ruler of all things is under no necessity to employ rare talents and acquirements in the course of His awful administration, but in the crisis of great affairs can lay aside a Pettigrew with as little concern as any other instrument, even the meanest.

Upon some fitting occasion no doubt his friends will see that the public is furnished with a more suitable and detailed account of the preparation he had made to do high service to his generation. It will then be better known that no vulgar career of ambition, and no ordinary benefit to his country, had presented itself to him as worthy of the aims and endowments of JAMES JOHNSTON PETTIGREW.

INDEX